“Ilene Lefcourt captures the essence of the complex a
tic process with parents, their babies, and young chil
hood memories to a central position and offers rich re
work to understand them. *Parenting and Childhood Mem*
exciting and accessible: a good combination of educati … otional support,
and psychoanalytic thinking.”
– **Christine Anzieu-Premmereur, MD, PhD**, Assistant Clinical Professor of Psychiatry, Columbia University; Director, Columbia University Center for Psychoanalytic Training and Research Parent-Infant Program

“In a lyrical, jargon-free style, Ilene Lefcourt gives us a highly original new book of parent-infant clinical stories. The case studies beautifully illustrate how parental childhood memories, out of awareness, trigger repetitions with the parent’s own child. As Lefcourt links these memories to current parent-child difficulties, parents come to have deep empathy for their children and themselves. And clinicians learn to become better clinicians. This book is a gem.”
– **Beatrice Beebe, PhD**, Clinical Professor of Medical Psychology, Columbia University Medical Center, New York State Psychiatric Institute; Author, *Infant Research and Adult Treatment*; *The Mother-Infant Interaction Picture Book*

“Ilene Lefcourt’s clinically nuanced case reports offer illuminating examples of our current scientific understanding of how memory is interpersonally co-constructed, and how it develops and transforms.”
– **Susan Coates, PhD**, Clinical Professor of Medical Psychology, Columbia University Center for Psychoanalytic Training and Research, Division of Gender, Sexuality and Health; Author, *Can Babies Remember Trauma? Symbolic Forms of Representation in Traumatized Infants*

“In this wise and riveting book, Ilene Lefcourt brings her vast clinical experience to life. Through discussion intertwined with rich clinical vignettes, she shows the power of the parent-child relationship as an agent of healing and growth. The intensity of the emotional experience of parenthood offers a unique opportunity to gain access to hidden memories both painful and pleasurable. By protecting time to listen to a parent’s story while observing their infant’s communication through behavior or their young child’s communication through play, Lefcourt creates opportunity for moments of meeting between parent and child that are transformative for both. Her ability to bring the reader into the complex and inherently messy world of parent-child relationships will be of value to parents and clinicians alike.”
– **Claudia M. Gold, MD**, Pediatrician, Boston Massachusetts; Faculty, University of Massachusetts Boston Infant-Parent Mental Health Program; Author, *The Power of Discord: Why the Ups and Downs of Relationships Are the Secret to Building Intimacy, Resilience, and Trust*; *Keeping Your Child in Mind*

"*Parenting and Childhood Memories* is filled with clinically moving stories about parents and their young children. Complex psychoanalytic principles and developmental concepts are illustrated in a clear and compelling way. A delightful read: mental health professionals and parents will be enriched by their own memories triggered and their insights acquired."
– **Irit Kushilevitz, PhD**, Assistant Director, Psychological and Developmental Clinic, Ministry of Health, Haifa, Israel

"Ilene Lefcourt's book is an important resource for pediatricians who are often asked questions about their patient's behavior and development. Through vignettes, and accompanying psychanalytic interpretations, Ms. Lefcourt provides a unique framework for understanding the deep connections between parents' own childhoods, and their interactions with their children. It is truly an important work."
– **Alanna Levine, MD**, Pediatrician, New York; Author, *Raising a Self-Reliant Child*

"This book is a gift to parents, mental health clinicians, and everyone interested in how we become who we are. It goes beyond 'how to' parenting advice to bring much-needed empathy for the inner world of parents, showing how their often-buried childhood memories re-emerge in how they perceive their children, and respond to the challenges of childrearing. In beautiful language, Ilene Lefcourt masterfully models how to promote the emotional growth of parents and young children by uncovering the links between the past and the present, to understand the meaning of seemingly inexplicable behavior problems, and to restore developmental health."
– **Alicia Lieberman, PhD**, Professor, University of California San Francisco, Irving B. Harris Chair in Infant Mental Health; Author, *The Emotional Life of the Toddler*

"Ilene Lefcourt offers us her astute and compassionate insights into the wonders and challenges of parenting. Her perspectives and gentle, thoughtful accounts of families inspire us to remember the magic of parent-child love and the way it can lead to growth and joy as well as layered meanings."
– **Catherine Lord, PhD**, George Tarjan Distinguished Professor of Psychiatry and Education, UCLA Semel Institute of Neuroscience and Human Behavior, David Geffen School of Medicine

"This book is as enchanting as it is serious and convincing. Ilene Lefcourt uses psychoanalytically informed interventions to help parents change the way they interact unconsciously with their children. The clinical vignettes that illustrate these interactions are arresting and moving. All readers are bound to embrace the wisdom of this book and be informed and changed by it."
– **Eugene Mahon, MD**, Private Child and Adult Practice, New York; Author, *Rensal the Redbit*

"Ilene Lefcourt brilliantly describes the powerful impact of insight, often only painfully acquired, for the benefit of parent and child alike. The author walks

the reader through a captivating collection of case studies that reveal the way in which our childhood experience shapes our relations with our own children. This book emerges as a remarkable and very readable analysis of family psychodynamics across generations."
– **Michael Meaney, CM, CQ, FRSC**, Professor, McGill University

"Ilene Lefcourt opens our eyes to an important part of the human experience: parent-child interactions and the development of the mind. Her understanding of this process is psychoanalytically informed and elegantly described. This book offers an opportunity to share in some of the most exciting experiences in becoming human. *Parenting and Childhood Memories* is particularly delightful as the author is both an empathic, talented clinician, and a skilled writer."
– **Robert Michels, MD**, Walsh McDermott University Professor of Medicine and Psychiatry, Cornell University; Former Training and Supervising Analyst, Columbia University Center for Psychoanalytic Training and Research; Former Joint Editor-in-Chief, *The International Journal of Psychoanalysis*

"This book should be read as a foundational guide for all those working with parents and young children."
– **Patricia Nachman, PhD**, Attending Clinical Professor, Mt. Sinai School of Medicine; Faculty, New York Psychoanalytic Society/Institute; Editor, *Daniel Stern: Contributions to Psychoanalysis and Developmental Psychology*

"Ilene Lefcourt has written a personal and elegantly constructed book about parenting and being parented, about being a child and growing up – the universal intergenerational impact of the past."
– **Rita Reiswig, MS**, Co-Director, The Anni Bergman Parent-Infant Program, Contemporary Freudian Society and IPTAR Psychoanalyst for Adults, Adolescents and Children

"*Parenting and Childhood Memories* is bewitching! Lovingly written narratives draw from the author's vast experience running an early childhood development center in New York City, treating and caring for families with infants and young children. These vignettes draw the reader in and enchant while at the same time, illustrating essential concepts in psychodynamic thinking about early parent-child relationships, formative development, and the many challenges infants, young children, and their parents face daily. This book is written in a way that is accessible to parents and professionals. Clinical observations are rich and nuanced in each chapter, which like fairytale classics, you will want to re-read again and again."
– **Daniel Schechter, MD**, Director, Perinatal and Early Childhood Ambulatory Care and Research, Department of Psychiatry, Lausanne University Hospital, Switzerland; Adjunct Associate Professor of Child and Adolescent Psychiatry, New York University Grossman School of Medicine

"Ilene Lefcourt convinces the reader that her urban enclosure is a magic and intimate place where secrets are revealed. A vast corpus of information about

development is woven in without pedantic ceremony. The kind of observations and listening that are required to achieve the outcomes illustrated are clear."
– **Theodore Shapiro, MD**, Professor of Psychiatry, Director, Infant Psychiatry Program, Weill Cornell Medicine New York Presbyterian

"Ilene Lefcourt brings to life both the child's and the parent's internal worlds and illustrates the crucial and sometimes magical process of giving and receiving love."
– **William Singletary, MD**, Child and Adult Psychiatrist and Psychoanalyst; Faculty, Psychoanalytic Center of Philadelphia; President, Margaret Mahler Child Development Foundation; Faculty, Psychoanalytic Center of Philadelphia

"Ilene Lefcourt's wise, warm, and erudite book is a work of love . . . always informed by her deep knowledge of psychoanalytic theory. . . . These stories will resonate with some of your own experiences as both a parent and a child, and you will discover universal, liberating truths about how we revisit our pasts."
– **Kerry Sulkowicz, MD**, President Elect, American Psychoanalytic Association; Clinical Professor of Psychiatry, NYU School of Medicine

"This wonderful book is perfect for anyone who was ever a child, anyone who wants to reenter and remember the magic of childhood experiences, stories, and emotions, and anyone who was, is, or hopes to be a parent. Understanding the impact of the past and its ghosts and narratives through Ilene Lefcourt's kaleidoscopic and spectral lens reveals the triumphs and tragedies of being a human raising humans. This compassionate and captivating condensation of 35 years of work with parents and children by a master clinician somehow manages to remain bewitching and transcendent in showing us who we are, who we are becoming, and why."
– **Susan Vaughan, MD**, Director, Columbia University Center for Psychoanalytic Training and Research; Author, *The Talking Cure*

"*Parenting and Childhood Memories* lends texture and meaning to intergenerational studies of parental bonding, brain development, and epigenetics. It translates into pathways of change when these relationships go awry. It is delightful to read and full of surprises to scientists and parents, and those of us who are both."
– **Myrna Weissman, PhD**, Diane Goldman Kemper Family Professor of Epidemiology and Psychiatry, Columbia University Vagelos College of Physicians and Surgeons

Parenting and Childhood Memories

Parenting and Childhood Memories is a collection of stories about the ways in which parents' childhood memories influence their current interactions with their babies and young children: the ghosts and magic of our minds.

This book explores the underlying meanings of parents' memories that emerge in their perceptions of their children and their responses to the challenges of early development and the everyday life stresses of parenting. Drawing on extensive material originating in mother-child groups and parent consultations, the author demonstrates that parents' emotional growth and ability to nurture their young children's emotional health is promoted by uncovering the links between the past and the present and unearthing the underlying meanings of seemingly inexplicable behavior. This original book, grounded in long-established psychoanalytic ideas, is about moments in early development and parent-child interaction that tell this story.

Offering useful insights, readers will be intrigued by the details of the therapeutic process described and be inspired by the outcomes. This book will appeal to psychoanalysts, therapists, mental health professionals, and parents.

Parenting and Childhood Memories

A Psychoanalytic Approach to Reverberating Ghosts and Magic

Ilene S. Lefcourt

LONDON AND NEW YORK

First published 2021
by Routledge
2 Park Square, Milton Park, Abingdon, Oxon OX14 4RN

and by Routledge
605 Third Avenue, New York, NY 10158

Routledge is an imprint of the Taylor & Francis Group, an informa business

British Library Cataloguing-in-Publication Data
A catalogue record for this book is available from the British Library

Library of Congress Cataloging-in-Publication Data
Names: Lefcourt, Ilene S., 1946– author.
Title: Parenting and childhood memories : a psychoanalytic approach to reverberating ghosts and magic / Ilene S. Lefcourt.
Description: Abingdon, Oxon ; New York, NY : Routledge, 2021. | Includes bibliographical references and index.
Identifiers: LCCN 2020044571 (print) | LCCN 2020044572 (ebook) | ISBN 9780367720681 (hardback) | ISBN 9780367720728 (paperback) | ISBN 9781003153313 (ebook)
Subjects: LCSH: Parent and child. | Early memories. | Parenting—Psychological aspects. | Psychoanalysis.
Classification: LCC BF723.P25 L44 2021 (print) | LCC BF723.P25 (ebook) | DDC 155.9/24—dc23
LC record available at https://lccn.loc.gov/2020044571
LC ebook record available at https://lccn.loc.gov/2020044572

ISBN: 978-0-367-72068-1 (hbk)
ISBN: 978-0-367-72072-8 (pbk)
ISBN: 978-1-003-15331-3 (ebk)

Typeset in Bembo
by Apex CoVantage, LLC

With deepest gratitude:

I thank my children, Jeff, Karen, Heather, and Ben. They navigate my ghosts magnificently and do parenting magic with my grandchildren. I thank my grandchildren, Kaia, Isaac, Violet, Clio, and Evelyn. They surround me with joy and fill me with contentment.

"I need a place where I can go,
where I can whisper what I know. . . ."

The Secret Garden
Lucy Simon and Marsha Norman

When Anna Freud was a young woman, and was looking for a job as a nanny before she had any work experience with children, she was asked by a prospective employer, "What qualifies you to be a nanny?" Ms. Freud answered, "I was once a child."

Psychoanalytic Lore

Contents

About the Author

Ilene S. Lefcourt established the Sackler Lefcourt Center for Child Development in New York City in 1982. For over 35 years she has been its director, provided developmental consultation to parents, and led mother-child groups with children from birth to 3 years. Ms. Lefcourt teaches child psychiatry residents and parent-infant psychotherapy trainees about her work. She organizes and leads professional workshops. Ms. Lefcourt is on the Margaret S. Mahler Child Development Foundation Board and is a faculty member of the Columbia University Center for Psychoanalytic Training and Research Parent-Infant Program.

> "Parents have questions and concerns about their children: personal insight often provides the answers."
>
> Ilene S. Lefcourt

Author's Note

In 1959, *The Magic Years* by Selma Fraiberg introduced parents and mental health professionals to an in-depth way to understand the developing mind of children: a psychoanalytic perspective. Mrs. Fraiberg's eloquent and evocative details of a child's inner world are as important today as they were then and are central to *Parenting and Childhood Memories*.

The early years of childhood can be viewed as magical because of the ways in which young children's minds work and the ways in which they see the world and themselves at each phase of development. The power of parent-child love and attachment is at the center of their world. Understanding their child's developing mind can help parents to decipher the underlying meaning of surface behavior, respond empathically, and promote development. These fundamental ideas are illustrated throughout this book.

Two articles also require mention: *Ghosts in the Nursery* (1975) by Selma Fraiberg, and *Angels in the Nursery* (2005) by Alicia Lieberman. Ghosts in this context are psychological remnants from parents' childhood experiences that influence parents' current interactions with their own children. Following are excerpts from *Ghosts in the Nursery*.

> "In every nursery there are ghosts . . ." "The baby makes his own imperative claim upon parental love, and the bonds of love protect the child and his parents against the intruders, the malevolent ghosts . . ." "Even among families where the love bonds are stable and strong, the intruders from the parental past may break through the magic circle in an unguarded moment, and a parent and his child may reenact a moment or a scene from another time."

Mrs. Fraiberg's seminal paper focuses on dangerous ghosts. These ghosts refer to the childhood trauma of neglect and abuse in one generation being repeated in the next generation. The mother's reactivated forgotten feelings of overwhelming terror are dangerously enacted with her baby. Inflicting the emotional and sometimes physical pain on her baby prevents the mother from feeling the pain herself.

Alicia Lieberman's important 2005 paper *Angels in the Nursery* expands Mrs. Fraiberg's ideas about ghosts by introducing the metaphor of angels. Dr. Lieberman draws attention to the importance of parents' childhood experiences of feeling understood, accepted, and loved. She highlights experiences of security and self-worth in the parents' past that influence their interactions with their babies and young children and promote parent-child interactions that lead to children's mental health. Dr. Lieberman beautifully describes this process:

> "self-affirming influences move silently in the lives of children, wrapping each successive generation in the security that comes from being loved, accepted, and understood."

Both Mrs. Fraiberg and Dr. Lieberman's ideas about the impact of parents' childhood experiences re-emerging with their own children apply to a universal aspect of parenthood. For most parents, childhood memories have complex combinations of loving and protective experiences and frightening, rejecting, and angry ones. Dr. Lieberman notes,

> "Ghosts and angels co-exist in dynamic tension with each other, at times actively struggling for supremacy and at other times reverting to a quiescent state."

In order to emphasize this fundamental internal mental process required for adaptation to the contradictory ups and downs of everyday life, and the love and anger in all relationships, I have chosen to call remnants of both kinds of childhood experiences by the same word, "ghosts." This underscores the important need and developing ability to mentally organize both pleasurable and painful experiences in ways that preserve a positive sense-of-self and the capacity for stable loving relationships. I define ghosts as relics of relationships from the past, traces of which are found in childhood memories and parent-child interactions: some pleasurable and some painful. The goal, for both parents and children, is for these conflicting mental representations to co-exist in ways that nurture the child's development and give adaptive meaning to parents' childhood memories.

Mrs. Fraiberg and Dr. Lieberman's ideas about children's developing minds, parents' childhood experiences, and parents' unique capacity for understanding are illustrated throughout this book.

Introduction

Parenting and Childhood Memories is a collection of stories about the ways in which parents' childhood memories influence their interactions with their babies and young children: the ghosts and magic of our minds. These are intergenerational tales about parents' childhood experiences that get repeated with their own children. Like photographs and family lore, the memories are handed down from one generation to the next.

The ghosts are relics of parents' relationships from the past. Their remnants are found in both childhood memories and parent-child interactions. The loving and protective ghosts co-exist, commingle, and sometimes clash with the angry and frightening ones. Often out of awareness, that is unconsciously, they whiz around playing peek-a-boo and influence parents' interactions with their children. Ghosts become known by the feelings they evoke, the interactions they embody, and the memories they trigger. All parents have ghosts. They sometimes bring joy and in other moments cause unhappiness. During the early years of parenthood, identifying and understanding the ghost shadows of the past can shed light on questions and concerns in the present.

The magic is parent-child love: the power it exerts and the discovery of self it engenders. Each story in this book describes a parent's journey from traces of a ghost that are causing unhappiness, to the emergence of a parent's childhood memory, to new self-understanding. Self-reflection leading to insight changes the meaning of the memory. When the meaning of the memory changes, feelings and interactions change. The reverse is also illustrated: changes in feelings, especially new feelings with babies and young children, promote self-reflection and transform the meaning of memories. Parts of memories that are hidden emerge. Parts that are disturbing grow dim. Parents' feelings of helplessness are transformed into action, uncertainty into confidence, and unknowing into understanding. These stories seem magical because parents with children under 3 years old are uniquely available to self-reflection and insight with deeper emotional significance than is usual at other times of life, and children under 3 years of age are easily influenced by their parents. Desired changes occur quickly. This is the magical power of parent-child love. I have highlighted moments in early development and parent-child interaction that tell this story.

In the hub of New York City, through a small courtyard lined with ivy, past a large delicately gated window, parents step into a place and time devoted to parents and young children. Through interior white shutters, they peek into a playroom: a dollhouse, wooden trucks, picture books, toys neatly arranged by category, and tiny chairs evoke vague outlines of childhood memories. While walking into the playroom with their babies and young children, parents' memories sharpen and the feelings aroused intensify. This is where these stories originated: the Sackler Lefcourt Center for Child Development. In a safe playground for ghosts to enter, the wondrous inner world of children can be known. Parent-child relationships can grow, childrearing approaches can be considered, and the personal meanings of memories can be elucidated. The questions and concerns that typically arise for parents in the first 3 years open the door to self-understanding. The fascinating and complex inner world of babies and young children, the meanings beneath the surface of parent-child interactions, and parents' childhood memories provide clues to the answers.

"We re-live our childhoods through our children" is an old adage that is often repeated. This statement characterizes the grip of parents' revived passions and the impact of parents' past experiences on their current interactions with their children. Re-living the past is conveyed in parents' comments: "Sometimes I sound just like my mother," or "I treat my daughter as if she's the mother and I'm the child," or "I've become the kind of father I always said I would never be." Re-living childhood refers to parents' ghosts being revitalized, and the intense feelings evoked. It also refers to the ways in which the past is being re-enacted in the present, sometimes without awareness. This is a universal aspect of being a parent.

The remarkable feeling of being transported back in time with their young children increases parents' self-reflection. Self-reflection helps parents to maintain their attention to both the surface behavior of their children and simultaneously to the underlying meanings. Babies and toddlers' thoughts and feelings quickly materialize into observable behavior. This close link between their inner world and their external behavior enables parents to recognize the increasingly complex, and at times contradictory, meanings of their children's behavior. A child's inner world includes the parent-child bond, feelings of security, sense-of-self, fantasies, wishes and fears, and the mental processes that lead to emotion regulation, frustration tolerance, impulse control, and the capacity to love. When children feel understood in terms of their wishes, the inherent conflicts between wishes (for example conflicts between pleasing oneself and wishes to please one's parents), and the evolving developmental resolution of conflicts, their development and learning are both promoted. Stories in this book illuminate this process.

Children's play is a special category of behavior. Like dreams and memories for adults, play provides a captivating glimpse into a child's wishes, fears, and conflicts. The fascinating details beneath the surface of behavior become visible.

Understanding what motivates their children's behavior and what it means is an essential ingredient of parents' empathy. Parents' communicating their understanding to their children is important because being known and feeling understood are at the core of being and feeling loved. We may not know what a baby is thinking, but what we imagine about their inner world informs our response and thereby contributes to the development of the baby's mind.

Parenting and Childhood Memories is based on a psychoanalytic approach to work with parents confronting their own personal ghosts in both mother-child groups and parent consultations. Parents' discoveries of new meanings of their children's behavior and their own, the childhood memories and insights that emerged, and the changes that occurred are described. The following are some examples. Cora's memories about separation from her own mother were preventing her from bonding with her 5-month-old baby until a dramatic moment of change was triggered (p. 6). Jesse's ability to remember his own painful feelings about saying goodbye to his father when he was a little boy enabled him to help his 2-year-old son with separations (p. 22). Roberta's 2-year-old daughter was hitting uncontrollably until the meaning of her hitting was understood (p. 44). Sally's memories about her childhood nightmares enabled her to help her 2-and-a-half-year-old son to sleep in his own bed (p. 79). Rose's confrontation with a painful part of herself that she struggled to hide enabled her to secure the bond with her 20-month-old daughter (p. 103). Other stories include themes of sibling rivalry, weaning, limit setting, potty training, and integrating career ambition with family life.

All stories have been disguised, and the details revised and fictionalized in order to protect the privacy of the actual parents and children. Some stories are composites. The statements quoted are paraphrases of actual statements. Some childhood memories reported are my own. Two goals are important: to ensure the privacy of the actual parents and children, and to tell stories that share the messages inherent in the original stories.

Just as my work with parents conjures up ghosts, perhaps childhood memories will be recalled and ghosts will be activated while reading these stories. This has been my own experience while writing them. These are not frightening ghost stories, but they may be disturbing. They may feel particularly unsettling because of the personal ghosts they awaken. Paradoxically, they may also seem like happily-ever-after stories and in some ways, they are. Parents' self-reflections may seem extraordinary, the changes that occur may seem sudden, and the insights that activate them unexpected. Internal shifts occur before changes that are observable. The changes illustrate the power of the parent-child love relationship that leads to the emergence of new feelings, new meanings, and new interactions.

It is impossible to identify the precise mechanisms of change or to predict how long the changes will last. Life-defining events that occurred in parents' pasts, even those that were difficult when they were occurring, created a context for resilience. Becoming a parent is a life-defining event with many stresses and profound pleasures: a new context for resilience that is easily activated.

The essence of what parents said to me and what I said to them is recounted throughout these stories; however, more than our words transpired between us. Parents are ready to enter into relationships that excite their curiosity about their child's developing mind and that heighten their own self-reflection. Parents and I create together a parallel relationship to the evolving parent-child relationship that provides a context for parents' self-discovery. Parents of young children are highly motivated to learn about the aspects of child development that are intuitive, counter-intuitive, and paradoxical. They learn from their parents, friends, books, professionals, and their own experiences. They learn from their children. They are vulnerable to criticism and hungry for support and validation. They are open to the exploration of their current interactions with their children, to the process of gaining insight about their childhood memories, to revived feelings, and to the creation of new meanings.

There are three categories of my interactions with parents: support, education, and the exploration, clarification, and interpretation of the underlying or unconscious meanings of parent-child interactions, children's behavior – including play – and parents' childhood memories. Vignettes illustrate a blending of these interactions. The parents that I work with are economically advantaged and highly educated. They are typical in that they want to be the best parents that they can be: like all parents they sometimes struggle.

While writing, I told these stories to my family, friends, and colleagues. I was moved and inspired by their eagerness and openness to tell me their own related stories. Frequently they told me about their childhood bunnies, teddy bears, and blankets. Some of their stories are included. Other stories I was told were about enduring painful memories: infertility, childbirth complications, postpartum depression, and breastfeeding difficulties. Even so, these stories were also infused with pleasurable enriching memories. Some childhood memories were filled with lasting relationship unhappiness, but also included in these stories was the healing that occurred with their own children. For some, the telling of events that took place decades ago seemed more like a re-living than a remembering. Sometimes new memories emerged as we spoke.

When the multiple meanings of memories are understood, both cognitively and emotionally, some elements that are vivid fade and other aspects that are hidden are discovered. Ghosts that are nurturing materialize and ghosts that are disturbing grow dim: feelings change. Parents' revitalized understanding of their own ghosts and parents' abilities to create new memories predict favorably for the next generation.

It is my hope that readers of *Parenting and Childhood Memories*, both parents and professionals who work with parents and young children, will become intrigued by their own childhood memories, their personal self-understanding will expand and the complexity and power of the parent-child relationship will be appreciated.

1 A Baby is Born

When a baby is born dreams of the future and memories of the past are awakened for the parents. Childhood memories are activated in interaction with their babies. Some memories emerge with a quiet murmur and others with a sudden jolt. Like the humming of a spinning-top and startle of a jack-in-the-box, they are distant reminiscences.

When parents hold their infants, feel their small warm bodies cradled gently in their arms, and breathe in their sweet fragrance, tender love may be aroused. When this happens, they are spellbound and remain transfixed. For other parents, or for the same parents at other moments, different kinds of memories are revived, and they freeze. Overwhelmed by the helplessness and vulnerability of their tiny babies and the enormous responsibility of being a parent, the changes in roles and identities, the sleepless nights and anxiety, they may feel helpless themselves and want to escape.

The origins of both of these reactions may not be obvious as they occur, but upon reflection can be traced to the parents' own childhood memories. Some cherished and others haunting, these memories contain parents' ghosts. All parents have ghosts that live in their childhood memories: love and understanding are the magic.

Parent-baby falling-in-love can be instantaneous or gradual. The process can be exquisitely subtle, breathtakingly intense, or anything in between. The falling-in-love experience for each parent and baby is unique. Cora and Lizzie's story that follows illustrates the impact of Cora's childhood memories and current interactions with her own mother on her relationship with her 5-month-old daughter, Lizzie.

Cora and Lizzie
"We are beginning to bond . . ."

It was a warm September day: a new year of groups was beginning. Bright sunlight was streaming into the playroom. Toy shelves the height of adults' knees, a yellow bin filled with small toys, and red cushions framed the interior open space. I was about to meet Cora and her 5-month-old daughter, Lizzie, who were joining a mother-baby group. I scanned the room to ensure that a safe, comfortable setting had been created for both the mothers and the babies; the familiar aroma of freshly brewed coffee filled the air.

Cora entered carrying Lizzie on her hip. Cora's crystal blue eyes peeked through her long, feathery bangs. Lizzie's body was wedged in the crook of her arm. I could barely see Lizzie's face. I led them past the white slatted shutters and through the waiting area where a photo collage of babies hangs on the wall above a pale gray banquette. We entered the mother-baby room; I sat on the floor next to the yellow toy bin. Cora adjusted her light beige gabardine suit, hiked up her skirt, kicked off her heels, and joined me on the carpeted floor. Lizzie was dressed in coordinated colors and wore a delicate baby-barrette to keep wisps of hair off her face. As Cora and I chatted, she propped Lizzie on the edge of her lap facing toward me.

Lizzie remained completely still, her rosy face unexpressive and her gaze riveted on me. She engaged me in intense and prolonged eye contact. The unusual pull from Lizzie for mutual gaze was so strong I struggled to maintain social eye contact with Cora. I wondered what it was about Lizzie, Cora, their histories, and current relationship that was contributing to these atypical patterns of interaction.

Our light conversation changed when Cora told me that she had returned to full-time work when Lizzie was 10 days old. Cora explained, "I'm different from most mothers. I'm like my mom, I work all the time. Sometimes I don't see Lizzie for four or five days." Underlying Cora's surface indifference to what she was describing seemed to be a suffering that was too painful to be acknowledged but was revealed in her next sentence: "When I do see her, she won't make eye contact. No matter what I do, she won't look at me." As we spoke, Lizzie's gaze remained focused on me. I was surprised by Cora's description and wanted to learn more. I asked, "How does it happen that you don't see Lizzie for four or five days?" Cora replied, "If I leave for work before she wakes up and return after she's asleep, I don't see her for days. When I get home and she's already asleep I think, why did I make my last appointment so late?" I probed further, "Why do you think she won't make eye contact with you?" Cora confided, "She's angry at me."

Cora was convinced that Lizzie was angry and that this was the reason Lizzie would not look at her, but she was unaware of the possible meanings of her belief. Cora may have had some anger toward Lizzie for not looking at her, but I thought this was secondary. More important seemed to be Cora's dawning self-awareness, though not spoken, that she was not only like her mother whom she had described as working all the time, but also that she was like she imagined Lizzie and had angry feelings toward her own mother. Cora's self-questioning about why she had been coming home too late to see Lizzie suggested her beginning self-reflection in addition to her self-blame. It also indicated a potential readiness to understand more about herself, including feelings of anger at her own mother. I focused on Cora's relationship with her mother and her childhood memories. I asked, "Who took care of you when you were a child?" Cora began, "Not my mother, other people. I remember when I woke up in the morning my mom was still asleep, and when I came home from school she wasn't there."

Cora's statement confirmed a connection between her childhood memories and her interactions with Lizzie. Although they occurred at different ages, the way in which Cora remembered the lack of contact with her own mother was almost identical to the way in which she described her lack of contact with Lizzie. "If I leave for work before Lizzie wakes up and return after she's asleep, I don't see her for days" and when talking about herself and her mother, ". . . when I woke up in the morning my mom was still asleep and when I came home from school, she wasn't there." The narrative similarities, the lyrics, and the music sounded as though they emanated directly from her unconscious. Cora was unaware of the similarities and what they might mean. Cora was convinced that Lizzie was angry because she was away at work, but omitted feelings connected to her memories about her own mother's absence. She stated that she wanted more eye contact with Lizzie and she questioned why she came home too late to see her. Hidden ghosts were beginning to surface.

As Cora and I spoke there seemed to be an absence of any emotional connectedness between her and Lizzie. Lizzie remained on the edge of Cora's lap facing away from her mother. They never looked at each other and were barely even touching. Lizzie was capable of eye contact; she was still seeking prolonged eye contact with me.

Cora went on to describe the physical distance combined with emotional closeness between her own mother and herself who had lived in different cities at opposite ends of the country since Cora was 16 years old. Cora explained, "I moved to New York with my dad, my mom stayed in Oregon to work." While Cora was describing the extensive physical distance between herself and her mother, she emphasized, "We are very close. We have a very intimate relationship. We talk on the phone every day." It seemed to me as though Cora's description of Lizzie avoiding eye contact was related to her childhood memories, as well as to her current feelings of anger and emotional disconnectedness from her own mother with which she struggled and was disavowing. At the same time, her desire for emotional connectedness with Lizzie was apparent.

I decided to point out the parallels between the absence of eye contact between Cora and her mother, and the lack of eye contact between Cora and Lizzie. I said, "You describe a very close, intimate relationship with your mother that takes place mostly on the phone. There is no eye contact possible on the phone. [This occurred before FaceTime.] When you and your mother are talking, you don't see each other. You also tell me about moments with Lizzie when you want her to look at you and there is no eye contact." Cora looked surprised with the connection I was making, but seemed to invite me to continue. She stilled, her eyes widened, and her shoulders relaxed indicating an internal shift. I wondered to myself whether Lizzie felt these changes. I continued, "It sounds like you want Lizzie to look at you and you want to look at her, but something interferes." I said to Lizzie, another way of speaking to Cora, "Mommy wants to look at you and mommy wants you to look at her." I did not expect what happened next.

At this moment, Lizzie twisted her entire body around to face her mother. It was unclear whether Lizzie rotated toward her mother and then Cora's arms embraced her, or Cora's arms embraced Lizzie first, and then Lizzie rotated toward her mother. Either way, Cora and Lizzie cradled in her mother's arms now faced each other and smiled in mutual gaze. They lingered for many moments in this shared pleasurable interaction of emotional connectedness. I talked to Lizzie again, "Mommy wants to look at you and you want to look at mommy." I said to Cora, "You have two important relationships without eye contact; we don't know what the connection might be between them. Maybe we can understand more about this."

The following week during the first mother-baby group, Cora told us, "Lizzie and I are just beginning to bond." The experience the week before of smiling in mutual gaze had kindled their falling-in-love; the kind of love that includes feeling emotionally connected. Cora experienced it as "beginning to bond." Thoughts of, I am your mommy and you are my baby; I love you and you love me emerged and began to consolidate.

It is not clear what had prompted the close body contact, intense mutual gaze, and shared smiles between Cora and Lizzie, or the feeling of bonding that Cora described. My comments had interpreted a connection between Cora's interactions with Lizzie and with her own mother, had been encouraging and gave permission, but the mechanism of change was imperceptible. Perhaps Cora felt seen by me in a way that she was only dimly aware of herself. I saw her as a mother who could connect with her baby, a mother different from her own mother. Cora's ghost memories related to her mother's absence had been entangled with the present in a way that interfered with her relationship with Lizzie. My comments and my beginning relationship with Cora had begun to disentangle them.

Babies are born ready to form attachments that include mutual gaze, shared smiles, and body closeness. Mothers and babies are highly motivated to connect, and mothers and babies are capable of dramatic changes. I have described an unexpected moment of connection between Cora and Lizzie: surprising when it occurred, yet consistent with theory.

As Cora participated in the mother-baby group, her childhood memories began to include feelings. She became aware of her conflict between being either like her mother as she described her, which helped her to feel closer to her mother, or different which helped her to feel closer to Lizzie. She began to feel increasingly gratified by her relationship with Lizzie, but sad and angry about the distance from her mother. Her impulses to escape from Lizzie faded. Cora found a new job with shorter hours. The meaning of her childhood memories had changed and new feelings emerged.

Typically, between adults, and between adults and babies, patterns of gaze and gaze averting fluctuate and are comfortable. When the gazers are in sync, there is a rhythm that is seamlessly smooth and goes unnoticed. When the rhythm or intensity is amiss, if there is too much avoidance of eye contact as it had been for Cora with Lizzie, or long stares as it had been for me with Lizzie, it is disconcerting. As part of their growing attachment and falling-in-love, parents and babies engage in pleasurable mutual gaze interactions. After Cora recognized how she was reliving her past with Lizzie, as well as repeating aspects of her current relationship with her own mother, loving moments of mutual gaze became possible. Feeling bonded emerged.

Parent-baby falling-in-love feels like a kind of magic. Babies have an innate readiness to form emotional attachments. Their maturational thrust augments this process. Babies establish relationship bonds with their parents that endure and confer security. Newborns orient to their mothers' voices and mold to their bodies. Infants are soothed by fathers' tender swaying embrace. Babies and toddlers seek proximity to their parents for safety and may cling when they feel safety is threatened. They also cling to parents for the pleasure of bodily closeness and emotional connectedness. Crawling babies stop in their tracks when their mothers signal danger. They squeal with excitement when their fathers throw them into the air. They point to things in order to entice their parents to experience a shared focus of attention. Babies and toddlers turn to their parents for information, comfort, and moments of shared pleasure. A special kind of falling-in-love is happening.

Babies' first smiles erupt spontaneously and delight parents. First smiles are fleeting, but captivating, and rich with uncertain meaning. A smile is an outward sign of an internal experience. First smiles invite parents to imagine the inner experience of their baby; their imaginings are part of the foundation of empathy and contribute to the baby's developing mind. Babies' early smiles stimulate parents' musings about what their baby is feeling and thinking; I know what it feels like to smile, they must be feeling something similar to what I am feeling. Early smiles activate parents' awareness of their baby's dawning consciousness. An emergent inner world of thoughts and feelings is glimpsed. It will develop to include you are my mommy, you are my daddy, I love you, and you love me. We both feel good while smiling with each other.

Babies' smiles quickly become interpersonal communications: an inter-subjective experience. The internal subjective experience of each is sensed by the other. Mutual gaze accompanies shared smiles and intensifies the experience. Parent-baby mutual smiles are interactive. The smile of each influences the smile of the other. They are silent two-way interactions, a kind of intense implicit conversation or improvised synchronized dance. During the first 3 years this connectedness deepens, intensifies, and sets in motion a capacity for emotional connectedness that continues throughout life.

Experiences of emotional connectedness are so robust they do not require sight. Sight is not needed for shared smiles. Inter-subjectivity does not require mutual gaze. A mother whose father had been blind since birth told me that her father always knew when she was smiling and smiled too. "He couldn't see me, but he knew me and loved me."

All love relationships have rupture and repair cycles. An important aspect of love relationships that young children and even babies are learning about is that angry feelings arise and that loving feelings return. Sometimes a rupture is repaired quickly and lasts only a moment. When parents say "No" and the baby startles or cries in anger, the rupture of loving feelings can be brief and repaired in a flash. With toddlers and older children, ruptures can be longer, the repairs may need to be more creative, and may require more steps.

When ruptures are repaired, smiles and caresses are restored. Later, when language is acquired, the words "I love you" reaffirm the bond.

Rupture and repair cycles of loving interactions occur in different ways. The next story is about a consultation with Kevin, who desperately yearned to restore his recently ruptured, mutually attuned, affectionate relationship with Suzy, his 19-month-old daughter.

Kevin and Suzy
"My little girl loves me again . . ."

I sat in my office, skimming a new journal while waiting for Kevin. Flanking the walls is a white filing cabinet, often with a stray mitten or sippy-cup on top, bookshelves, and two bulletin boards with holiday photos of Center families. For over 30 years, prominently displayed above my desk is a small, framed collage with delicate fabric cutouts of six little hands: 1985 is embroidered on the top. The parents in a mother-baby group gave the collage to me as we said goodbye for the summer.

At exactly 5:30 Kevin arrived. He swaggered in with a lit cigarette dangling from his lips. A small scar on his forehead appeared through his gently tousled hair. Kevin loomed big and imposing in my otherwise comfortably crowded small office. He was about 6' 2", wearing blue jeans with a large brass buckle on his belt, and an opened white shirt stretched across his slightly protruding paunch. A gold link necklace rested on his exposed chest. He had an intricate tattoo on the inside of his wrist. Kevin was an English professor and a bundle of contradictions. I invited him to sit in the chair next to mine and asked him to extinguish his cigarette. Kevin winked at me and crushed it between his fingers.

Kevin was consulting me about his 19-month-old daughter, Suzy, who recently began to "reject" him. He described sadly, "Lately, Suzy always pushes me away when I try to kiss or hug her. When she was a baby, we were very close. I was the only one who could soothe her in the middle of the night. I think she felt so secure in my arms. Dada was her first word." Kevin's impassioned longings and inspired description of his interactions with Suzy when she was a baby emerged through his rough exterior, "I love her and want us to be close." While talking about Suzy, Kevin interjected memory snippets about his own father, who frequently hit him when he was a boy. The most horrifying part about Kevin's memories was that each time he was going to be hit, he was required to select the belt from his father's large collection that was kept on a revolving rack. This detail focused my attention on Kevin's metal belt buckle, perhaps a remnant of a ghost.

As we spoke, Kevin increasingly cursed and lapsed into tough-guy colloquialisms. I suspected that his tough-guy exterior was constructed in an attempt to ward off attack and humiliation that seemed to be triggered when I asked him to extinguish his cigarette, and when he crushed it with his fingers. I found his fluctuating harsh and gentle ways poignant and engaging.

In order to understand more about Kevin and Suzy's relationship, I asked Kevin to describe how he and Suzy played. He began, "We play this great game. I growl and chase her. She squeals and runs away and I catch her. It's great fun. Suzy loves it, we do it over and over." I talked with Kevin about the growl and whether Suzy while appearing to love the game may also be scared by it. I wondered to myself whether Kevin's cursing was a way to growl at me.

I asked Kevin about the origins of his chasing game with Suzy. I was surprised by how aware he was about the derivation of the game. Kevin explained, "When I was a kid, the school bus dropped me three blocks away from home. I played this game that a tiger was chasing me. I had to run home as fast as I could and get in the door before the tiger got me, which I always did." I said, "It sounds like a scary game with a happy ending – you escape the tiger." "Yeah!" he boasted with a broad smile. I added, "It seems like you are now playing a new version of the old game with Suzy, only you're playing a different role. You are now the scary tiger and Suzy is the frightened child being chased. There is another big difference in the game; Suzy gets caught by the growling tiger." Kevin looked surprised, taken off guard, and intrigued. For a moment he looked stuck between the interplay of his childhood ghosts and his adult tender longings.

Kevin and I talked about the ways in which his game as a child had enabled him to escape in play what he could not escape in actuality. As a child, the tiger game had helped him to cope with the frightening painful beatings he received from his father and the humiliating, sadistic ritual of being forced to choose the belt. The meaning of his memories about his childhood game expanded to include its protective purpose and the sense it fostered of his being in control.

A week later, Kevin called to thank me. With the new meaning of his tiger ghost, and in the context of feeling more lovable and safer, Kevin had stopped playing the chasing game with Suzy, as well as other games with the same frightening theme. Suzy began to welcome Kevin's gentle hugs and kisses as in the past. Once again, they began to enjoy loving moments of shared smiles and mutual gaze. The rupture in their loving interactions had been repaired.

As a grown man, Kevin was no longer being hit. He was a tenured professor with a lovely wife and little girl. He no longer needed the new version of the old game. It embodied a remnant ghost that his self-reflection and insight allowed him to discard. Kevin's tough guy demeanor, which sometimes got him into trouble, would require more understanding to relinquish.

Memories of childhood games including tickling, rough-and-tumble play, variations of I'm going to get you, and boo are vivid. The feelings about the games are sometimes conflicted. Some childhood memories of rough-and-tumble play with siblings and with parents may be pleasurable as a distant memory; however, names like tickle-torture and descriptions of being completely overpowered and pinned down, and feeling angry and helpless convey ambivalent feelings about the play. The warning "This will end in tears" is often heard from bystanders and captures the fragility of the pleasure in this kind of play.

Tickling and rough-and-tumble are special categories of play. Included are swinging children around by their arms and legs, throwing them up in the air and catching them, hanging them upside-down, and many forms of wrestling. There are various kinds of tickling: gentle fingertip stroking of skin that evokes intense sensory pleasure and deep tickling that triggers explosive uproarious laughter. These kinds of high arousal games are exciting and typically part of parent-child play. They increase in intensity during the first 3 years and serve a developmental and relationship function. Sharing body pleasure is part of intimate relationships. Losing control that requires trust of the other is part of the play. Pleasurable and satisfying intense arousal is a valuable human experience: being able to enjoy it and to return smoothly to a state of equilibrium is an asset.

The excitement of high arousal games for both parents and children can be intoxicating. Yet, while experiences of highly stimulating play can be valuable to children within the safety of their parents' presence and embrace, if the intensity is too high or too frightening there can be unwanted results: for example, when children bite in this context it is an indication that the play is too intense and the children are overwhelmed. Sometimes genital arousal occurs. A mom once told me about a nighttime ritual of gently fingertip tickling her daughter's arm, back, and tummy before sleep, as she had been tickled. One night, pointing to her genitals, her 2-year-old daughter said, "Mommy, tickle me down there." The mother was startled. She had not realized that the tickling was arousing "in that way." Regulating optimal arousal levels internally and interpersonally is a necessary part of the play.

A major element of the inner experience of high arousal play is sensorial; the excitement of the room seeming to spin, the disorientation of being flipped upside down, the thrill of almost falling and being caught are riveting. In addition to body sensory experiences and altered states, there are thoughts, emotions, and fantasies for both parents and children that are part of rough-and-tumble play and tickling. The physical experience is so intense that the symbolic or emotional meaning of the play often remains in the background.

There are aspects of high arousal play that are shared by all parents and children; however, each parent and child have their own unique version including the frequency, intensity, parts of the body touched, how the play is initiated and terminated, and the ways in which each individual responds to touching and being touched, the specific sounds and smells. As with all play, the uniqueness and specificity of each particular relationship are part of the pleasure. As is suggested by my description, there are some parallels between high arousal play for children and sex for adults.

2 Childhood Memories and Ghosts

Childhood memories are a fundamental part of mental life. They are mental constructs related to actual events and include associated wishes, fears, conflicts, and feelings. Explicit memories of events are created and organized into narratives. They are crafted portrayals of experience that illuminate the personal meaning of events. Other memories are not organized into narratives. They are implicit memories: for example, memories of the experience of shared smiles, hugs, loving, and feeling loved. Angry and frightening experiences can also be remembered implicitly. Implicit memories can be retained in painful or pleasurable sensory experiences: body sensations including tastes, scents, sounds, and emotions – shivers, quivers, and swoons. Other implicit memories are related to ways of being with another: turn-taking rhythms in conversation, patterns of mutual gaze and gaze averting, touching, being touched and avoiding touch, falling-in-love. Parents' implicit and explicit childhood memories shape their relationships and are prototypes for their behavior with their children. Parents' childhood memories about events at a specific age can be triggered and enacted with their own children who are at a different age. Memories condense and encapsulate a multitude of meanings: conscious and unconscious. Remnants of ghosts, that is, representatives of relationship moments from the past, reside in childhood memories and like dreams, the memories can be interpreted and understood.

A mother once asked me, "Why do my sister and I remember the same childhood event so differently?" I replied, "Memories are personal creations. Differences in memories of the same event contain information about the meaning the event has for each individual: how the event relates to each one's past experiences, fears, wishes, and ways of adapting. Siblings have different experiences with their parents and different memories of their parents. Each parent-child relationship is unique."

Disturbing ghosts inhabit the frightening, humiliating, sad, guilty, shameful, envious, and angry childhood memories. Some ghosts feel dangerous and are difficult to confront. They reside in memories that include receiving harsh punishments, physical and emotional. They linger in memories about being criticized, excluded, or rejected. Childhood memories about separation and loss are ubiquitous and may contain ghosts that invade parent-child sleep routines. Ghosts sometimes surround mealtime, and the attendant battles about what children eat and how much. Memories of wetting pants and the shame or punishment that follows may emerge when parents teach children to use the potty. Taking children to the doctor can evoke parents' memories of painful and frightening medical experiences. Some memories activate the lasting guilt from childhood in response to having teased and tormented a sibling, or having been teased. They can have an impact on parents' reactions to their children's sibling rivalry. Sometimes ghosts are reminders of painful childhood memories that motivate parents to be different than their own parents. Other memories that contain disturbing ghosts relate to family secrets and trauma that get passed from one generation to the next: for example, the lingering impact of the childhood death of a sibling.

Disturbing ghosts are suspended in time and like the cuckoo that bursts through the background ongoing tick-tock, they are expected but may still startle and intrude. "My child knows how to push my buttons" is everyday vernacular announcing that ghosts have arrived. Insight can transform them.

Cherished ghosts also live in parents' memories: nurturing, protective, and loving childhood memories that include feelings of joy, self-worth, safety, agency, and pride. These ghosts usually influence most of what occurs between parents and their children. They flicker in and out of conscious awareness. They may easily evoke pleasurable feelings and confer resilience during stressful events. Other times they are hidden and difficult to access but can be re-awakened or created by parent-child interactions. Some ghosts represent ideals. Sometimes the ideals are impossible to emulate and result in feelings of inadequacy. Mostly, ghosts contribute to the ever-present intuitive, empathic, and supportive responses of parents to their children. The joyfulness elicited when a baby smiles may be evidence of the evocation of pleasurable, ghost-filled childhood memories. A re-awakened childhood fantasy of the wished-for parent sometimes provides a helpful ghost. Ghosts may shape family rituals that are passed from one generation to the next. Cherished ghosts fuel growing parent-child love and attachment. They also help parents to tolerate the significant stresses of having babies and young children. Cherished ghosts quietly hover, tumble in when needed, and infuse the motivation and capacity for parents to understand their memories, gain insight, and promote empathy.

Some childhood memories about playing may be filled with feelings of contentment, a sense of self, and aliveness. These memories are not populated with ghosts. There is no anger, fear, love, conflict, or wish central to the memory. Body exhilaration or mental excitation is the main experience in these memories. Childhood implicit memories of jumping rope, zooming around on a bike, or getting lost in a book can evoke a core sense of self-vitality, and elicit a strong sense of the continuity-of-self. And while change is characteristic of development, a simultaneous sense of the continuity-of-self is also needed. A young child's beginning continuity-of-self was revealed when 4-year-old Tania, in anticipation of swinging on a high circus trapeze, said, "I've wanted to do it my whole life."

Cherished and disturbing ghosts co-exist in childhood memories. Both are essential. They mingle and can be entwined. They are easily activated at family celebrations and during times of adversity. Childhood memories are often child-like. They are fanciful, allegorical, metaphorical, and at times whimsical. They can be illogical, contradictory, and absurd. In these ways they are dream-like. When childhood memories and their ghosts are viewed through an adult lens, particularly through an adult parent lens, they are thought about differently. A parent's perspective that applies maturity, logic, and reason changes their meaning. The love that parents feel for their child, self-reflection, and insight transform them. Ghosts are potential protection for the next generation. Loving and caretaking ghosts help parents to nurture their children. Hurtful and rejecting ghosts alert parents that introspection is needed.

A mother once told me that she created a baby diary not only to record her son's developmental milestones that she wanted to be sure to remember, but also to document how difficult a baby and toddler can be. She wanted a written record of the stressful times because she believed that pleasure and love would predominate her memories. While she was talking about the intermingling of her cherished and disturbing memories in the future, I wondered how pleasure and pain co-existed presently in her memories, and what experiences from her past were not being remembered.

In the next story, one of Blair's pleasurable memories about her mother was reawakened when Kyra was born. Unknowingly, acting out the memory was interfering with Blair's mourning and 2-month-old Kyra's age-appropriate growing alertness and beginning play in the mother-baby group.

Blair and Kyra
"I want to be a mother, but sometimes it's so sad . . ."

Pleasurable memories are sometimes enacted to substitute for or to ward off associated painful memories. Like the sticky push and pull of marshmallow taffy, a parent may get caught in a time warp between memories of the past and the present moment. For Blair the pull was toward painful grief, and the push was toward pleasurable memories of her mother and moments with her baby. The security and support in the mother-baby group enabled Blair to tell her story and to mourn.

Kyra was 2 months old when she and Blair joined a new mother-baby group with six mothers and their babies 2 to 5 months old. The mothers and I sat in a circle on the carpeted floor. While the babies sat on their mothers' laps or lay on blankets, their babbling and cooing could be heard through the din of our voices. It was a lively group with bubbling discussions about the amazement and delights of infant development, and the particular stresses for parents during this phase. The mothers were close observers of the week-to-week changes in their babies. Each woman was discovering the uniqueness of her baby and of herself as a mother. The babies were thriving. As the weeks passed, the mothers were feeling less stressed and more competent. Sleep routines were becoming more stable and predictable. Smiles were being enjoyed. Mother-baby play was flourishing. As the babies in the group approached 4 to 7 months old they were alert, beginning to sit, roll on the floor, and to explore the mother-baby playroom toys. The older babies were beginning to crawl. Kyra was different.

Week after week, throughout each group Kyra slept nestled under a soft, pink cloud of cashmere against her mother's body, embraced in her mother's arms. Both Blair and Kyra seemed completely content with this cozy arrangement. I wondered about its meaning. When asked, Blair had always noted, "This is a good time for Kyra to sleep."

When Kyra was approaching 5 months old and was still sleeping throughout the group, I asked Blair again whether our group met at a time when Kyra usually slept. This time Blair had a different answer indicating her readiness for insight. She was calmly reflective, "No, this is not her nap-time, but I like Kyra sleeping on me like this during the mother-baby group. It feels just right." I thought more details would help us to understand the meaning of this sleep pattern. I asked Blair what she liked about it. She self-reflectively replied, "I like the way her body feels. I like the feeling of her weight on me, warm and still. I can feel the rhythm of her breathing – the gentle bursts of her breath on my neck, her heartbeat. It feels good." Blair seemed to be capturing in her carefully chosen words the specifics of an experience from long ago: fragments of a distinct body sensation memory. An implicit memory seemed to be emerging and coming into focus. Because the details were so specific, I asked Blair if what she was describing reminded her of anything. She thought for a moment and then said, "When I was 3 years old my mother had a stroke and became paralyzed."

Blair remembered being cared for by her maternal grandmother after her mother's stroke. Everyday throughout her childhood, she was taken to visit her mother. Blair fondly remembered the details of being placed on top of her mother's reclined, immobilized body. We discovered that for Blair, the memory of these visits with her mother when she was a child and Kyra sleeping on her body during the mother-baby group were related. The implicit pleasurable body memory of being with her mother was being re-enacted with Kyra.

Blair's mother had died three years before Kyra was born and since her birth Blair was missing her mother in a way that she had not before. Blair reflected, "I want to be a mother, but it's so sad sometimes." Kyra sleeping on Blair throughout the mother-baby group and Blair feeling her breath and heartbeat were ways to feel close to her own mother rather than experience the intensified painful feelings of loss since she became a mother herself. At the same time, this sleep pattern was interfering with Kyra's age-appropriate alertness, social interactions, and play during the mother-baby group. It was also preventing Blair from sharing moments of this developmental phase with the other mothers.

After connecting Blair's memories about her own mother and her intensified grieving since Kyra was born to Kyra's sleeping during the group, there was a change. The specifics of how this change occurred are not known; nor is it known how the sleeping pattern between mother and baby had been created or sustained. The next time the mother-baby group met, Kyra awoke for the last 15 minutes. During the following group she was awake for the last 25 minutes, and at the next group Kyra remained awake throughout the entire time. Now rather than sleeping, Kyra began to manipulate toys, squeal and kick with delight, and observe the other babies. She had a glowing smile and was beginning to sit. Blair and Kyra maintained emotional connectedness while at a slight distance through mutual gaze, shared smiles, and gentle caresses. At times Kyra sat on her mother's lap smiling, observing, or interacting with the other babies. At other times, she lay on her pink blanket, excitedly kicking and rolling over. It is true that Kyra was now older and needed less sleep. However, something else also seemed to be happening.

Blair was a doctor and had a busy work schedule before maternity leave. She believed she had decided to become a doctor because of her mother's stroke and the disabilities her mother had suffered. Being a doctor had always helped Blair to feel close to her mother. Blair recalled, "After my mother died, I buried myself in work. I was ok. But since Kyra's birth, I miss my mother more. I especially think about her all the time when I'm here, in our mother-baby group."

Blair described her intensified grief with each developmental step Kyra took. She had reactions not only to the loss of the younger baby Kyra had been, but also to the renewed waves of sorrow related to her mother's disabilities and death. She was deeply saddened that her mother would not know Kyra at each developmental stage, and witness and share each achievement. Blair's sadness about her mother missing Kyra's life activated memories of parts of her own childhood that her mother had also missed. This additional insight about feeling sad about the parts of her own life that her mother had missed was another aspect of the past that was unknowingly being repeated. She had thought she was only sad about her mother missing parts of Kyra's life and realized that she was also sad about the parts of her own childhood that her mother had missed.

Renewed mourning with each of Kyra's emerging maturational milestones was signaled by a subtle gesture from Blair that presented a slight impediment to Kyra. For example, when Kyra was beginning to crawl, Blair placed her in the center of her encircling legs, creating an obstacle to crawling. Blair and I became able to recognize this pattern together. On the threshold of each developmental step, we began to anticipate her revived mourning that triggered the impulse to create an impediment for Kyra. We could talk about the painful feelings of loss instead of Blair acting them out with Kyra. The mothers provided additional support and shared with Blair the pleasure in Kyra's development. When Blair's childhood memories of her mother were now activated, they could elicit bearable sadness instead of being denied by her clinging to Kyra.

Many years later, Blair called to tell me that Kyra had graduated college and had been accepted to medical school. Together we had navigated the pleasures of Kyra's early developmental achievements and Blair's associated grief. We were both moved by this shared moment.

Implicit childhood memories can be retained in pleasurable or painful body sensations. They are stored in different parts of the body: in sounds, tastes, and smells. When evoked, they are difficult to organize into words. A swoon triggered by a fragrance, or a shudder in response to a sound, may be the rumblings of an implicit memory. The associated feelings may be communicated to the baby as they were in the prior story about Blair and Kyra.

The personal meaning of a memory that is organized into an explicit memory narrative can be understood. What triggers the memory, what it represents, and what is disguised in the memory can be revealed. The details of the memory, or parts that seem incidental, can have important meanings. Feelings expressed by one person in the memory can substitute for feelings of the memory's creator. A pleasurable part of a memory can disguise painful parts. Elements of a memory can have symbolic meaning. Memories are ways of coping with stressful events and processing and preserving pleasurable ones. As emotionally painful as memories can be, they may be a defense against even greater, unthinkable pain. Some memories fade and change over time; some remain fixed. Others are easily and frequently triggered. The following story about Jesse and Tyler has examples of these memory permutations.

Jesse and Tyler
"Saying goodbye is hard . . ."

It was a late Friday. I was rushing to leave my office when the phone rang. "It's Jesse, Tyler's father. I'd like to schedule an appointment. Lately Tyler cries too much, he cries all the time. He's not a baby anymore." Tyler was 2 years old. He and his mother Marianna had been in a mother-child group since Tyler was 6 months old. He was a thriving little boy with a cheerful disposition. Marianna had mentioned Jesse's concern, and I had expected his call.

The following week as I waited for Jesse to arrive, I opened my morning mail, glanced at the newspaper, and straightened the array of papers on my desk into neat stacks. Jesse entered my office carrying what looked like his morning coffee. He wore an elegantly tailored, stone-gray suit complementing his distinguished graying hair. A refined silk tie completed his polished appearance. Jesse looked like the success he had become. We settled quickly, sitting opposite each other in front of my desk. I pushed a tray of crayons to the corner of the desk to make room for Jesse's coffee.

After a few social exchanges about the frosty weather and the first snow flurries of the year that had just begun to fall, Jesse told me how difficult it was when he left his wife and son each morning to go to work. "I'm very busy. I don't have time for Tyler's tantrums." The frostiness of the weather was mirrored in Jesse's surface attitude toward Tyler.

Jesse then went on to explain that every morning before leaving for work, his wife Marianna, Tyler, and he always enjoyed a leisurely, sumptuous breakfast. It ended with freshly baked warm popovers sprinkled with powdered sugar. Jesse gravely emphasized, "I arrange my schedule to have this special breakfast together, but then it's time for me to leave. I don't have time for his tantrums." The co-mingling of Jesse's ghosts was eloquently revealed, and the tension between them clearly drawn. Some ghosts were linked to separation, and other ghosts to sugar popovers.

After a brief pause to gather his composure, Jesse continued, "Every morning after this happy breakfast together, when it is time for me to leave, as I pick up my briefcase and walk towards the door, Tyler begins to cry. He chases me to the door and clutches my leg. As he clings and screams, Marianna unlatches his strong grip." I wondered if the details of Jesse's description indicated some identification with Tyler's experience. However, Jesse remained decidedly disapproving of Tyler for being such a "crybaby" and blamed Marianna for "babying him." "He's a big boy now. He needs to learn he can't have everything he wants."

As we spoke, I highlighted how much Tyler loved him, and how sad it was for him when his daddy was leaving. I added, "Tyler wants you to know how he feels." I also noted that while Tyler's language was well developed for his age, he was telling his father how he felt in the best way he could. Remembering Jesse's statement, and wondering what he might himself be struggling to accept, I added, "It takes a long time to learn you can't have everything you want." At this moment, Jesse recalled a memory about his Sunday visits with his own father after his parents had divorced. It was a vivid memory that he frequently recalled.

Jesse was 10 years old. He remembered ice-skating, gliding over the ice, faltering where the ice crumbled, and trying to make turns the way the older boys did as they zoomed by. The rink was crowded with parents holding children's hands and couples dancing together – Jesse skated alone. His father remained outside the rink, turned away, a hazy image in the distance. His sister, too young to skate, watched from a bench. Each Sunday after ice-skating, before saying goodbye to his father and before returning home to his mother, Jesse always ate a powdered sugar doughnut: sometimes two. Jesse's description of the delicious sweet taste and smooth texture of the powdered sugar melting on his tongue was enticingly specific.

Jesse clearly remembered a particular Sunday when his father had driven him and his sister home after ice-skating. It was time to say goodbye. Jesse was standing alone in the doorway watching his sister with tears streaming down her face run up the street chasing their father's car. As he drove away, she screamed, "Daddy, daddy come back!" Jesse told me that he frequently recalled this memory.

The explicit, most vivid-feeling parts of Jesse's memory were his own sensory pleasure, eating the sugar doughnuts and his sister's emotional pain crying for their father. I asked Jesse, "What might be the connection between these two intense feeling parts of your memory?"

As Jesse and I talked, he realized that the memory about his sister's emotional pain was a way of remembering his own warded off feelings, however sweetened by the sugar doughnuts and distanced by his crying sister running away. Jesse now recognized that in his memory he had attributed to his sister his own sad feelings and his wish to cling to his father.

Jesse connected this insight about his memory to his morning goodbyes with Tyler. He realized that as a child he had felt the same way as Tyler. Jesse could now remember his own sad feelings rather than displace them onto his sister, try to obliterate them with sugar, or relive his denial of them with Tyler. The sad little boy beneath the cool, manly exterior was revealed, not only to me, but also to himself. The surface ice was crumbling. The warmth of his love for Tyler flushed his cheeks.

I commented, "In your ice-skating memory you make two references to being alone, ice-skating alone and standing in the doorway alone." Jesse then told me about his fear that he and Marianna would divorce and he would be alone. In some ways, saying goodbye to Tyler each morning triggered memories of his repeated goodbyes to his own father, his father's emotional distance and preoccupations that had left Jesse feeling alone in his father's presence, his chronic feelings of aloneness with his mother, fears about getting divorced and being alone again, and his continued struggle to accept that you can't have everything you want. Jesse then described how alone he had always felt when with his mother. He attributed this to his mother's angry outbursts, emotional coldness, and unavailability. Jesse linked his disapproval of Tyler's separation behavior to his self-disapproval for his own feelings about separation, loss, and aloneness.

With these insights, Jesse began to help Tyler to talk about his sad and angry feelings about saying goodbye. They began to play a variety of hide and seek games, and other games of separation and reunion. Jesse also told Tyler that when he was a little boy he cried when it was time to say goodbye to his father. Jesse and Tyler created new goodbye routines that included a special family handshake. The family continued to eat sugar popovers together. Separations between Jesse and Tyler became easier for both of them.

Jesse's memory had evolved. It expanded to include more of his feelings. The original elements of his memory remained: they included the slick, cold surface of the ice that crumbled under his skates, his father's rejection and unavailability, and the sweet sugar doughnuts. The memory of his sister crying in anguish as she ran up the street became blurry. The meaning of his memory had changed. Revealed under the crumbling surface of the ice was Jesse's loving warmth and empathy. Jesse was no longer rejecting his own sad feelings and his wish to cling to his father. He acknowledged his memories of his own father's un-empathic rejecting behavior, but also memories of his father's love. He connected his fears of being alone to the extent of aloneness he experienced with his mother. He conveyed an acceptance of Tyler's feelings that melted the frost between them and made separations easier. The speed and extent of Jesse's insight and the changes that followed are striking. They illustrate the power of the loving parent-child relationship and parents' unique capacity for self-reflection and insight when their children are young.

Separation reactions begin to occur when a baby develops an attachment to a parent. Reactions to separations continue throughout life. Parents' separation reactions, conscious and unconscious, latent and expressed, influence how they help their own children to cope with separation. Separations can be stressful: they can trigger strong protests or the reactions can remain internal. Both are meaningful. Children need to adapt to separation. Their relationship with their parents and their developing internal image of their parents will influence how they react to separations. Parents' will influence how their children adapt. Saying goodbye and play related to separation can help children to cope.

Peek-a-boo, a classic game initiated by parents and passed down for generations around the world, is understood to be a game of separation and reunion. It delights babies because it helps them to practice with pleasure something that is stressful: separations from mommy and daddy. They are learning that mommy and daddy still exist when not seen and that they return. Toddlers and young children play hide and seek, a variation of peek-a-boo. These frequently repeated games with parents provide opportunities to master separation and reunion in a playful context where separations are brief, and reunions are joyful. After playing such games with parents, children create their own versions of the games to further their learning. They may hide objects between sofa cushions, or delight in the pleasure of a toy that can be kept concealed in a pocket and revealed at whim.

When Sabrina was 10 months old, after having played various forms of peek-a-boo with her mother and father, she developed her own version with a ball. While seated on the floor, she flung a hard ball that fit perfectly in the palm of her hand across the room with all her might. Sabrina was a petite little girl, but the ball flew forcefully, fast and far. Scooting across the room, she then quickly retrieved it. This game of object permanence, and separation and reunion with the ball, was endlessly repeated for many weeks. She learned that the ball existed even when she didn't see it. She could always find it even if it rolled under the sofa, which was especially delightful: she would lose sight of it, re-find it, and retrieve it herself. An additional part of the pleasure in Sabrina's game was that she herself had initiated the separation from the ball, and unlike when separated from her parents, which they had initiated, she also controlled the reunion. When separated from her parents, she needed to wait for them to return; when she was separated from the ball, she had caused it and she could also get it back. Sabrina's parents supported her play even though it was more suited for the playground. They understood its importance. Original play created by a child to master a stressful actual event has enormous learning power.

Parents' experiences of separation and loss, whether remembered explicitly or implicitly, consciously or unconsciously, are significant to the ways in which they negotiate separations with their own children. Parents' childhood memories of separation and loss are often filled with ghosts. Trudy and Grayson's story that follows is an example.

Trudy and Grayson
"I'm remembering things I never knew . . ."

Sitting in my office between mothers' groups, I received a frantic call from Trudy. "My son Grayson has been waking every night for the past two weeks, screaming for hours, nothing soothes him. He's 2-and-a-half years old. I'm exhausted and worried. His pediatrician examined him and said he seems fine. My friend Ursula said maybe you could help." Trudy mentioned that there had been no changes to trigger Grayson's night screaming, but in passing remarked that she and her husband had been away for a few days. Trudy's apparent denial of the significance of this separation from Grayson alerted me to its possible importance. Trudy's distress seemed urgent. We scheduled an appointment for the next day.

I met Trudy at the door and escorted her into the sitting room that adjoins the playroom. Soft, pale gray banquettes create comfortable seating for parents. Trudy chose to sit equidistant between the toy-filled play area and me. Frequently gazing at the toys as we spoke, it seemed as though she was envisioning Grayson with us and childhood memories were being awakened. Trudy was a quiet, gentle woman with a graceful, artistic look. She worked as a theatrical make-up designer. Her soft, prematurely graying hair was swept up into a loose ponytail with untied wisps framing her face and twisting down her neck. Her long, printed skirt draped over her legs.

Trudy described Grayson's inconsolable crying and flailing for hours in the middle of the night. "Nothing soothes him. He just screams, glassy eyed. It's like he doesn't recognize me. He looks terrified." Emphasizing the panic she was feeling, Trudy added, "It looks like he's having a seizure." While Trudy and I talked about Grayson screaming in terror, she mentioned again with the same apparent disregard that she and her husband had been away for a few days. The contradiction between her simultaneous denying any significance to it, while at the same time repeating it, alerted me further to the possibility that separations had specific meaning to Trudy. I was not surprised by Trudy's answer to my next question. "Did Grayson know you were going away? Tell me about the goodbye." Trudy explained, "We didn't tell him. We don't want to make a big deal about separations. They go easy for us. Parents make too big a deal every time they go out. Grayson is fine with separations." This suggested to me that separations and goodbyes might be a big deal for Trudy. She continued, "I never say goodbye when I go to my studio, out for the evening, or away for the week. We never call when we are away."

Trudy's consistent denial of the significance of separations and any associated feelings was notable. Her rejection of the importance of Grayson knowing what to expect was concerning. For a young child, an inability to recognize and to share feelings, or to know what to expect, specifically about separations, can create anxiety, confusion, and inner turmoil that might result in nighttime screaming devoid of content, sometimes referred to as night terrors.

I wanted to understand more about what separations were like for Trudy when she was a child. I asked, "What were goodbyes like in your home growing up?" Trudy began, "My parents went away all the time. It was always fun. One time my mother was in the hospital for a month when I was 6. She always went away. I don't remember why or what it was like." As Trudy talked about childhood separations, her narrative became increasingly disjointed and contradictory, with repeated references to not knowing. Since this narrative pattern sometimes indicates unresolved trauma, I gently commented, "You don't want to make a big deal about separations from Grayson, but it sounds like separations have been a big deal for you."

Trudy then told me that both her parents had died in a car accident five years earlier. "I don't know any details about the accident. I never wanted to have children. Children can ruin a marriage, but after my parents died we decided to have a child. Not that you should try to replace someone you love with someone else. I had a friend who remarried after her husband died. If you really love someone you don't replace them." In the midst of her passionate, but somewhat fragmented and disconnected comments, her ideas about "replacing someone with someone else," "children can ruin a marriage," and "I don't know any details about the car accident" got my attention. I wondered how these ideas might be related to Trudy's general denial of feelings and to Grayson's night screaming. I also wanted to understand more about Trudy's feelings of guilt that might be contained in her statement about replacing someone you love.

Trudy's childhood memory fragments about separations and vague information about her parents' deaths seemed linked to her interactions with Grayson, but it was unclear how. It also seemed as though separation and loss had merged for Trudy and may have contributed to her wish to deny the significance of separations. Trudy's stream of reminiscences also suggested a possible connection between her distress and Grayson's, her dawning awareness of a connection, and a readiness to explore it.

I reflected on what Trudy had told me. I said, "You've experienced a lot of loss, not always with goodbyes." Trudy continued, "My mom went away for two months when I was 10 years old. I don't know why. I don't know much about my childhood." Thinking about her frequent references to not knowing, I remarked, "It sounds like there is a lot of not knowing." Trudy went on, "I have no memory of playing with my mother. I don't know how to play with Grayson. I got strong messages from my mom that motherhood doesn't fulfill you." As we spoke, I felt moved by Trudy's confusion, aloneness, and sadness that perhaps had resulted in a profound emotional disconnection from Grayson.

I shared my ideas. "It sounds like when you were a little girl your thoughts and feelings were not acknowledged, or even known." Trudy responded, "We never talked about feelings in my family." I added, "A child can feel frightened and very alone without words for feelings and someone to share them. Creating memories becomes more difficult." We went on to talk about Trudy's grief reactions to her parents' deaths. I noted to myself that her comments about her parents were exclusively positive. Since all relationships have both pleasurable and painful parts, this was noteworthy.

I talked to Trudy about the importance of saying goodbye to Grayson, and explained the usefulness of playing games of separation and reunion: games like hide and seek. I also described huckle-buckle-beanstalk: a game where an object is hidden in plain sight. The hidden object is visible, but is not readily seen. In a way, this game parallels the experience of acquiring insight: thoughts and feelings that are disguised, hidden, or denied become known. Trudy's feelings beneath the surface were beginning to emerge. I described sleep as a kind of separation and the kind of goodbyes that are related to sleep that might be useful, for example, bedtime routines including a goodnight song or story.

While Trudy and I talked about her thoughts and feelings, including how much they were not talked about when she was a child, she continued to deny that Grayson had any feelings about separation, or about anything. She was unaware that her conviction that Grayson did not have feelings was a repetition of her own memories about her childhood that were devoid of feeling. I became convinced of the extent of Grayson's emotional impoverishment without words for his feelings or their acknowledgment. His inner world was completely denied. I wondered how this inner emptiness might be connected to his uncontrollable nighttime screaming.

Although Trudy continued to deny Grayson's feelings, she was beginning to talk about her own. I repeatedly challenged her denial of Grayson's feelings and suggested that his night screaming might be related to thoughts and feelings that he was having during the day. I wanted to evaluate Trudy's ability to work with me. I said, "We can work together to better understand Grayson's feelings and also to help him to know them." I wanted to be clear about the process and goals that our work together would include. I added, "Grayson needs ways to think about his thoughts, feelings, and worries, and ways to communicate them during the day. During the night his thoughts, feelings, and worries will become organized into dreams and will enable him to sleep." While I was talking about Grayson, I was also talking about Trudy. In some ways this was an overflowing first meeting, but Trudy seemed ready.

I met Grayson two days later. He was a physically well-developed little boy: tall and robust, with thick, dark hair cut in a classic style. We stepped into the playroom. A light wood table with eight small chairs, a bookrack, and a chalkboard were in the far corner. Toy shelves lined the perimeter. A large window overlooking the entry courtyard let light pour in. I placed several small cars on the carpeted area in front of a toy shelf, put together a wooden road, and opened the sandbox. I suggested that Trudy and Grayson play together.

Trudy and Grayson slowly and quietly sat on the carpet next to the road. Grayson appeared anxious: his own play was inhibited while he closely monitored his mother and attempted to please her by following her lead. Trudy elaborated on Grayson's subtle play gestures with her own fantasies. For example, when Grayson tentatively placed a car on the road, she embellished his play, creating a three-car collision. When Grayson began digging in the sandbox, Trudy began burying the baby dolls. Grayson soberly played along. Trudy's play themes were exclusively funereal. Car accidents, death, and burials predominated. Death, a final separation, seemed central to Trudy and provided the main content of their pretend play together. Trudy's play contrasted sharply with her repeated denial of the significance of separation. While playing, both Trudy and Grayson appeared emotionally flat: strikingly devoid of obvious feeling. As we left the playroom an outpouring of urine gushed down Grayson's leg, streaking his pants, soaking his shoes and socks, and perhaps revealing a flood of feelings he could not contain.

I decided to schedule our next appointment without Grayson. It seemed to me that Trudy needed to talk about the separation and loss themes that had dominated her play with him. Meeting weekly, for the next three weeks Trudy and I talked about many of her daily interactions with Grayson. I supported her focusing on him and her emerging interest and understanding of Grayson's inner world of thoughts and feelings. This promoted her growing awareness of and pleasure in Grayson's attachment to her that had previously been ignored and denied. Trudy's questioning and challenging the evidence of his attachment to her had been related to her earlier comments, "If you really love someone you don't replace them, children can ruin a marriage, and motherhood doesn't fulfill you." For the moment, these more complex themes and the ghosts that surrounded them were left unexplored. Instead we talked about Grayson's everyday 2-and-a-half-year-old feelings of frustration, fear, anger, and at times, sadness. We began to talk about how Grayson might feel about separations from her, and her feelings about separations from him.

Trudy's idealizing statements about her own parents and husband became more balanced with some angry, disapproving ones. Most important, as we began talking more about her feelings, Trudy started to talk to Grayson about his feelings. This is an example of the parallels between my interactions with parents and their emerging interactions with their children. Trudy began acknowledging life events that affected Grayson. She initiated a bedtime routine and began to say goodbye to him. Trudy was relieved to tell me, "Two nights last week Grayson did not awake screaming; he slept till morning."

The frequency of Grayson's night screaming had begun to diminish. Trudy now reported that Grayson was wandering around the house in the middle of the night. Making a prediction that I could not be certain would occur, I told Trudy, "When Grayson is able to tell you more about his concerns and worries during the day, he won't wander around in the middle of the night. Instead, he will come to you." Trudy's next statement reassured me about my prediction. She said, "Grayson began talking in his sleep. In the middle of the night he says, 'No sleep, no bye-bye.'" I remarked, "Grayson may be telling you in the middle of the night what's on his mind during the day. He's not able yet to tell you 'no' during the day. Can you tell me about times, in addition to separations, when he may feel like protesting, but doesn't?" Trudy was now able to begin to reflect on the myriad moments during the day that Grayson might feel angry, sad, worried, or simply disagree with her. Trudy seemed struck with a new idea. "You mean the things that are on his mind during the day have been waking him up at night."

The following week, Trudy told me about a prior pregnancy that ended in a stillbirth. "I had excruciating pain everywhere. I was bleeding, hemorrhaging. I was terrified." I extended her comments to include Grayson. "You had your night of terror and Grayson is now having a kind of night terror."

The next week when Trudy and I met, she told me that Grayson had only three nights of waking and screaming. She continued to talk about the stillbirth. "When I was in the hospital and the baby had already died but was still inside me, the doctors would come in and listen for a heartbeat. There were new doctors all the time. They didn't know my baby had died. For 15 minutes, every time they would try to find the heartbeat. I couldn't stand it, finally I would tell them my baby died. They were horrified and apologized. It happened over and over." I said, "It sounds as though each time this occurred you re-lived the experience of first learning that your baby had died." Trudy responded, "Yes, I was learning it again and again for the first time." Thinking to myself about the reasons Trudy kept repeating this experience, I added, "I wonder if in those 15 minutes while the doctors were trying to find the heartbeat whether you thought maybe they would. You were not yet ready to say goodbye." Trudy replied, "Maybe I wished they would. Since I've been seeing you, I tell Grayson goodbye whenever I leave him and I talk to him about his feelings. He likes talking about feelings. My husband and I used to talk and cry every night about the baby who died. We don't talk about it anymore. I never told my friends the details; they wouldn't want to hear them. I didn't think I was still thinking about it. I'm remembering things I didn't know."

Trudy was able to talk with me about things that had been unseen, unspeakable, and unknowable. Her comments seemed to be oblique references to her self-accusations about "replacing someone you love with someone else." I thought that she was alluding to her self-disapproval about loving Grayson who had replaced the baby who had died, who had replaced her parents. We did not make these details explicit but uttering them even obliquely may have helped her to complete the mourning process and to be able to have an emotionally empathic relationship with Grayson. The following week, Trudy told me that there had been no night screaming. Grayson was now sleeping through the night. The night screaming never returned.

I was stunned by Trudy's statement, "I didn't think I was still thinking about it. I'm remembering things I didn't know." Her words exquisitely capture aspects of mental functioning: the paradoxes of simultaneously knowing and not knowing, forgetting and remembering. Trudy's statement suggested her beginning ability to understand and accept the complexities of her own mind and memories.

Trudy's comment about not talking with her husband about the baby who died since Grayson was born had reminded me of her earlier statement: "If you really love someone, you don't replace them." She had been talking about adults remarrying after they are widowed, but I wondered in what ways she felt Grayson was replacing the baby who had died, and whether her horror and guilt about that idea was contributing to the denial of feelings, her own and Grayson's. There was more to understand, but the night screaming had stopped. Both Grayson and Trudy's inner worlds of thoughts and feelings were now more organized, structured, and accessible. Trudy's ghosts that had created blueprints for denying her own and Grayson's feelings were now relegated to being memories of the past.

Trudy's fragmented childhood memories, devoid of feeling and filled with not knowing, had been enacted with Grayson. The expectation that motherhood would not be gratifying, the recent sudden deaths of both her parents, the stillbirth of her first born, Grayson's night screaming, and her concern and love for Grayson coalesced in a way that made change necessary and possible. Solutions like denying feelings and not saying goodbye that may have been adaptive earlier in her life had led to an emotional disconnect from Grayson. Trudy's awareness of the gaps and inconsistencies in her childhood memories, her memories about the stillbirth, and the parts she told to me that she thought nobody would listen to, her new understanding about Grayson's needs to know his feelings and to share them with her, and most importantly the changes in her relationship with Grayson, enabled Trudy to think about her memories differently. Trudy was now able to say goodbye to me.

Childhood memories about the birth of a sibling have an impact on parents and the ways in which they talk to their children about sex, pregnancy, and childbirth. Children are interested. They pay attention to what is told to them explicitly and to what is communicated to them implicitly. Children add their own theories to the information given to them and fill in the gaps created by omitted, difficult to understand, or emotionally laden information. Children have reactions to their mothers' pregnancies. Age, birth order, and gender influence their reactions. Mothers' feelings about their pregnancies and about having another baby also have an impact. Children may react to their mothers' pregnancies with changes in their eating patterns or use of the potty.

Central to all memories are feelings. Sometimes the feeling parts of memories are less accessible, as they had been for Trudy in the previous story. Sometimes feelings predominate as in the next story about Elise and Ajax. Elise was pregnant with her second child. Her intense feelings and painful memories related to her own sibling rivalry were having an impact on her interactions with her son Ajax, who was 36 months old and had stopped using the potty.

Elise and Ajax
"Mommy, I have a baby in my tummy . . ."

A mother-child group was about to start. The mothers and their children gathered in the waiting area next to the white slatted shutters. At 9:30 I opened the door. The children grabbed their jackets, ran through the mothers' room into the playroom, and hung them on their colored hooks. As they began to play, a gentle hum filled the room. The women settled onto the banquette. I took my usual chair next to the door.

In the midst of a lively discussion about toilet training, Elise mentioned, "Ajax just is not into it anymore; I think I'm going to put him back in diapers." Ajax was now 3 years old and had been using the potty for 3 months. He wore underpants all the time. Two days earlier he had stopped using the potty: he refused. The women were surprised. Ajax was a verbal, competent little boy, and learning to use the potty had gone smoothly for him. I wondered what the connection might be between Elise being 8 months pregnant and Ajax beginning to protest any use of the potty. I also wondered what the connection might be between Elise being 8 months pregnant and her apparent nonchalance about Ajax refusing to use the potty.

Elise had been a preschool teacher and recognized the value of talking to children about the expected birth of a sibling. She frequently read her favorite children's books on the subject to Ajax. She had carefully selected them because they included information about babies and being an older brother. Elise emphasized the beautiful illustrations of older brothers feeding, helping to change diapers, and playing with the babies. She also highlighted that the books portrayed babies crying, making a mess, and taking space on mommy's lap. Elise believed Ajax was well informed and prepared for the arrival of his baby sister. I wondered what Ajax was being told about his mother's pregnancy and what he thought about it.

My next comment added a ripple to our discussion, "Regardless of what information young children have been given about pregnancy and childbirth, they may have their own theories about who can get pregnant, and how a baby gets in and how it gets out of mommy's body. When mothers are pregnant, their children Ajax's age, boys as well as girls, often have thoughts and feelings about a baby being inside their own bodies – just like mommy. Children may think that a baby can get in if they eat something and get out when they poop. This has been their own experience with things getting in and out of their bodies. They also know that everyone eats and everyone poops. With the data they have, their theories make sense." The women remained quiet and curious. Ajax was the oldest in the group; two other children were also in underpants, and another mother was pregnant.

I asked Elise about Ajax's reactions to this phase of her pregnancy. Rejecting the connections I was beginning to make between her pregnancy and Ajax refusing to use the potty, she asserted, "He's never said anything, we just read the books. I don't think he thinks about it." I suggested that, "Sometimes children communicate ideas or fantasies they have about pregnancy through their play. For example, they may put a pillow or stuffed animal under their shirts." Elise said she thought "It would be weird for Ajax to do that," and then said, "I want Ajax to feel that the baby is his baby too. I don't want him to feel displaced by the baby as I did by my sister. I just don't talk about it."

Elise's memories about feeling displaced by her sister were motivating her interactions with Ajax. Her solution to ensure that Ajax would not feel displaced by the baby was for him to think, "the baby is his baby too." I wondered whether this idea had translated for Ajax into "there's a baby in my tummy too," and this idea was interfering with pooping in the potty.

I began to question with Elise whether her wish for Ajax to feel "it's his baby too," and her concern that he would feel displaced by the baby as she had felt by her sister, might motivate her to communicate ideas to Ajax that he could misinterpret as there is a baby in his tummy. Elise appeared thoughtful, but did not say anything. An internal shift seemed to be occurring. (Because Ajax was going to have a baby sister, I thought about whether the idea that there was a baby girl in his body had also triggered gender-related worries about body parts and body products that intensified his refusal to use the potty.)

The following week Elise reported that "Ajax played being pregnant for the first time. He stuck out his tummy and said, 'I have a baby in my tummy.'" Elise took the opportunity to clarify for him, "The baby is only in mommy's tummy. You will be the big brother." Maybe coincidentally, but maybe not, the next day Ajax resumed pooping in the potty.

It is not clear whether Ajax had played being pregnant before, but his mother had never noticed; or whether Elise communicated something different to Ajax that enabled him to clarify something in his own mind that then triggered his play. Or perhaps hearing us talk during the mothers' group had been useful to Ajax. For Elise, the image of seeing Ajax pretending to be pregnant allowed her to differentiate her wish that Ajax not feel displaced by the baby, from a fantasy that he was pregnant. She also understood the importance of Ajax making this distinction. Ajax's ability to play being pregnant revealed in a clear way some thoughts that were on his mind of which his mother had been unaware. Elise agreed that what Ajax was thinking might be related to pooping.

Ajax's play that revealed his fantasy of being pregnant triggered a change in Elise's solution to her concern that Ajax would feel displaced by the baby as she herself had felt when her sister was born. Her solution was no longer "it's his baby too." Elise shifting her focus from feelings about her sister, and perhaps her own childhood fantasies, to Ajax's inner world and how his thoughts and feelings about her pregnancy were linked to his pooping behavior enabled her to help him.

3 The Inner World of Children

The inner world is the mental realm where memories dwell: where wishes, fears, and ghosts reside. The inner world of children is a magical world where parents' kisses soothe the pain away and teddy bears are a child's best friend when parents say goodbye. The power of parent-child love is at the center of their world. Being understood is at the core of being and feeling loved.

Parents' surprising discoveries about their child's inner world are reflected in the images of the children's awe when Mary Poppins reveals her needed and treasured items taken from what appears to be her empty carpetbag. This image is vivid and enduring because it resonates with the shared need of children and adults to feel deeply understood beneath the surface. For children it includes the need to be known not only as the child they are, but also as the child they are becoming.

The inner world is a metaphor for each person's subjective perceptions that reflect the external world, and include their associated thoughts, feelings, and conflicts. Parents' recognition and acknowledgment of their child's inner world promotes the parent-child bond and the development of the child's sense of self, impulse control, frustration tolerance, the ability to regulate emotions, and the resolution of universal developmental conflicts: for example, the conflicts between attachment and autonomy, and self-pleasures that conflict with relationship pleasures. Attention to a child's inner world is essential for parents' empathy. Attributing phase-specific developmental meanings to a child's external behavior enriches parents' ability to empathize.

Play is a window into the inner world of babies and young children. Understanding the meaning of play initiated by children enables us to understand more about what is on their minds: their feelings, worries, wishes, conflicts, and developing sense of self. (This was seen in the prior story about Elise and Ajax.)

Children play to learn and for pleasure. Play with mommy's earrings, daddy's tie, or their keys – objects the baby seems to mentally associate with a parent but are not actually part of the parent – expand the baby's inner world. The importance of the object to the baby seems to be beyond its intrinsic properties of texture, scent, or sound. The pleasure in touching the object, the significance of the object to the baby, it's meaning, is established by the baby. The baby associates the object with the parent. This kind of mental process may be a precursor to the baby's mind becoming part of their sense of self. With older babies and toddlers this is seen when they develop an attachment to a treasured toy and endow it with soothing capacities that give the object its value, and when an older child asserts, "It's my idea, don't copy me" or "I thought of it first."

Play enables babies and toddlers to have an impact – to make things happen. Play with rattles, blocks, and puzzles enhances children's feelings of agency and effectiveness: a sense of "I can do it." While still small, they can make big things happen. They can shake a rattle and make a sound, bang a ball and make it come out of a hole, or turn a knob and make a clown pop up. They can erect a tall building, knock it down, and build it again.

Pretend play is a way to master stressful events like going to the doctor, or to do things in fantasy that cannot be done yet in actuality, such as driving a car. As previously illustrated by Sabrina's beginning symbolic ball play, (p. 25), play can help to master separation. While playing, children can feel masterful and in control. Their inner worlds can develop.

Beginning mirror play can reveal a dawning new perspective of self, a developing component of the inner world. A mother sent a video to me of her baby's self-discovery during mirror play. Dakota had a full-length mirror in her bedroom. When she was younger and her mother held her in front of the mirror, Dakota seemed to focus on looking at her mother's reflection. When she was 11 months old, sitting on the floor in front of the mirror, Dakota did something different. Anticipating a moment of discovery, her mother watched excitedly through her iPhone camera from across the room.

Very close to the mirror – almost touching it, for several moments focused and still – Dakota looked carefully at her own reflection. She then stuck her tongue in and out slowly and deliberately several times. Her concentration intensified. Her eyes widened. She then moved her head gently towards the mirror, all the time looking attentively until her forehead touched the mirror softly. Her forehead remaining on the mirror, Dakota paused and scanned her reflection. Her mother said, "Yes, you see your nose." Dakota wiggled her nose and then moved her forehead away from the mirror and again forward to touch it, slowly and gently. She then repeated ever so slowly sticking her tongue in and out several times. Next she gently and seemingly knowingly put her lips on her mirror image and kissed her reflection. Her mother joyfully commented, "You are giving yourself a kiss." Dakota turned away from the mirror and looked at her mother with a big smile.

Dakota's new mirror play demonstrated an emerging expanded sense of self: herself seen from the outside while experienced on the inside. Her mother watched with delight. Dakota's process of learning about her mirror image, her inner experience of wonder at her discovery, and her pleasure sharing it with her mother were visible on the video.

Body play begins young. Three-month-old infants discover their hands and repeatedly wave them in front of their eyes. They discover that their hands are always there, and they can make them appear and disappear from sight. Their hands become part of their sense of body-self that they can control.

Soon after, they discover their feet and in time their entire bodies. Babies and toddlers have no inhibitions about body exploration and body pleasure. Children's body play often surprises, delights, and sometimes embarrasses parents.

Body play with parents includes pleasurable touching, kissing, and labeling body parts: the child's and the parents. Parents choose which body parts are ok to touch, to kiss, and to name, which body functions such as sneezing, coughing, passing gas, and pooping are ok to talk about together, and which body differences can be acknowledged – skin color, hair texture, eye color, hair color, gender, and idiosyncratic differences. The body words parents choose to teach their children, what bodily functions they talk about, and how they talk about them are related to their own childhood memories, and their adult attitudes about sex, gender, and race. For example, a mother once told me, "I know most people teach their children the word 'vagina.'" With a shudder and look of embarrassment, combined with excitement, she added, "I can't do that. My mother never used that word." I said, "It seems like it sounds too sexy to you. You don't want to think about your little girl that way."

When children become interested in the naked body, undressing dolls may become a frequent play activity. When Harper was 2 years old, her older sister introduced her to female Polly Pockets, which quickly became her favorite doll. Polly Pockets are glamorized realistic miniatures with a collection of tight-fitting, stylish outfits. The clothes are so tight that Harper could not dress the dolls herself. Her pleasure and favorite activity was undressing them. Harper's other passionate activity was adorning herself with prototypic female accessories: headbands, tiaras, sparkly shoes, and bracelets. She would wear only dresses. She was making a strong statement: "I am a girl." Her gender focus on herself and her play undressing the dolls appeared to be related. Both seemed connected to her emerging and consolidating female gender identity. She had an idea about what girls look like on the outside; she wanted to know more about what they looked like under their clothes, maybe even on the inside. Her parents supported her play. They struggled tirelessly to dress and re-dress the dolls so Harper could undress them, again and again.

Intrinsic to development is change, internal and external. During the first 3 years of life some changes are gradual and some occur in leaps. Internal changes result from the evolution of mental processes in response to maturation and to experience. Parents' interest and attention to the underlying meanings of their child's behavior, and communicating their understanding to their child, promotes the child's self-reflection, frustration tolerance, emotion regulation, and growing awareness of their inner world, and the inner world of others. In this way the internal changes in a young child are entwined with parents' understanding of their child's developing mind.

In the following story, Taylor's understanding of 15-month-old April's inner world was communicated symbolically to her through doll play. Their beginning mother-daughter doll play promoted April's social referencing, feelings of safety, emotion regulation, and the ability of both mother and toddler to feel connected with each other in the playroom.

Taylor and April
"I need to be held too . . ."

April was 15 months old. Her hair was neatly held in two short ponytails with yellow ribbons. In her plaid skirt and stylish boots, she ran stumbling forward to catch up with her mother, who was entering the mother-toddler playroom. This was the second time the group was meeting. Taylor, April's mother, quickly joined the other mothers huddled together on red cushions. The mothers were eager for the pleasures of adult female companionship in the sea of toddler dirty diapers and temper tantrums. April, alone as she crossed the threshold, looked adrift.

While the mothers were commiserating about the difficulties navigating the city with little children and warding off the advice and criticisms of strangers, the children played. Some children stayed close to their mothers, one remained on her mother's lap, and others played at a distance, periodically touching base. Either a glance across the room, a quick hug, or a shared play activity with mommy enabled the children to resume their independent play, or to join a group activity.

April and Taylor were different. April barely played. She whimpered as she wandered aimlessly around the room. It seemed as though April did not have the needed beginning formation of an internal image or sense of her mother, or sense of self-with-mother, that could enable her to feel emotionally connected when at a slight distance. She neither stayed close to her mother, nor did she use mutual gaze in order to feel connected, safe, and comfortable when at a distance. It was as if she were alone in the room with no one to whom she could connect. When on a few occasions April dropped a doll next to her mother and then walked past her, perhaps an indirect way of giving the doll to her mother, Taylor seemed not to notice. When April dropped the doll in her mother's lap, Taylor removed it from her lap and placed it on the floor.

After observing this pattern several times, I wanted to interest Taylor in the possible meanings of April's behavior. I commented, "Children use play to learn and to communicate. When a child gives something to mommy, it means something." I asked Taylor, "What might it mean when April gives the doll to you, or drops it next to you, or in your lap?" Taylor was interested and asked me, "What could April mean?" I continued, "I wonder if April wants to watch you with the doll so she can feel something about what it's like to be close to you: to feel secure. As she explores the toys and interacts with the other children, she may need to be reminded what it feels like to be held by you, and to feel safe." In response to my implicit suggestion, Taylor grabbed the doll, though roughly, and held it awkwardly.

I had piqued Taylor's curiosity and awakened related childhood memories. During the next mothers' group while sitting close to me, Taylor talked about her frightening memories of her father's rages, and her mother's fear and helplessness. Taylor described one night when her father threw a lamp at a window. Her mother screamed. Splintered glass scattered the floor. Taylor was not sure if the light bulb or the window had broken, but she remembered feeling terrified.

Taylor continued to sit next to me during each group, perhaps feeling in some ways held and protected by me. April increasingly handed the doll to her mother and watched as her mother increasingly held the doll gently, embraced it tenderly, and protected it from the other children who wanted to take it. April began to sit on her mother's lap. Her mother cuddled and caressed her.

The parallels between my interactions with Taylor, the ways in which Taylor held the doll, and the interactions between Taylor and April were striking. April and Taylor's doll play, qualitatively and functionally, was similar to my interactions with Taylor. As Taylor sat close to me, I listened to the details of her childhood memories of terror which she now felt safe enough to describe. When across the room from her mother, April was no longer distressed. She felt held and safe watching her mother tenderly hold the doll. April's independent play had become more organized and focused. She was now able to both initiate physical contact with her mother and connect with her emotionally from a distance.

April and Taylor were now able to connect both physically and emotionally through mutual gaze and shared smiles. This kind of shared implicit experience of knowing: I see you, you see me, you are thinking about me, I am thinking about you, you are safe, we are emotionally connected, has been described as social referencing. It is an inter-subjective interaction, a kind of emotional connectedness through mutual gaze when at a physical distance. In these ways, both physically and inter-subjectively, April refueled; she filled up with momminess.

Social referencing and proximity seeking are typical of toddlers' attachment to parents. They are also triggers for parental ghosts. April had not yet been able to achieve these developmental milestones reliably. For Taylor, frightening feelings and memories had been triggered by April's needs for closeness and protection that interfered with needed mother-toddler interactions. It seemed as though Taylor did not hold April physically or emotionally in the mother-toddler room because in some ways she had felt so un-held herself. Taylor had been re-living with April aspects of her own childhood memories about her father tormenting the family with his rages while she felt unprotected, alone, and un-held by her mother.

Taylor understood that April needed to feel held, emotionally connected, and safe. Holding the doll was a symbolic substitute, a kind of doll play that began the process of Taylor and April feeling emotionally connected in the playroom. The doll play promoted mother-toddler physical closeness, and social referencing when at a distance. Holding the doll and sitting next to me seemed to also help Taylor to feel held and safe herself. Taylor was now able to remember her aloneness and terror, without re-living it.

The inner world of children is understood through identification and empathy. It is aided by knowledge about child development. Parents' own childhood memories fortify the process. Parent-child love and attachment enhance the ability of parents to empathize with their children. The converse is also true: parents' empathizing with their children intensifies parent-child love. Being and feeling understood is one of the most powerful aspects of feeling loved.

Learning to talk also requires being understood. Often parents are the only ones who understand their toddler's emerging language. When parents are uncertain about the meaning of their baby's utterance, they rely on the context to attribute meaning. The baby's approximation of a word, in combination with the parent's enunciation of the word and attribution of meaning to it, creates a new word for the baby. In this way, the language acquisition process is about communication between parent and baby; it is an interpersonal process about feeling understood and meaning making.

When babies begin to point, they orchestrate a shared focus of attention, a meeting of minds, a kind of empathy and emotional connectedness. Initiated by the baby with a physical gesture, the inter-subjective experience of pointing can be written as:

> Baby pointing, I see that
> Parent, I know you see that, I see it too
> Baby senses, I know, that you know, what I see
> Parent is aware, I know, that you know, that I know.

Babies and young children seek to maintain emotional connectedness in different ways at each phase of development, in each specific context. Toddlers explore the world with feelings of emotional connectedness: the secure base parents provide. (This was seen in the previous story about Taylor and April's emotional connection through doll play that promoted physical touching and social referencing; p. 38.) Building on mutual gaze and shared smiles, the next developmental step in the discovery of feeling emotionally connected is pointing and the shared focus of attention it creates. Social referencing during limit-setting interactions is an elaboration of mutual gaze and pointing: it creates a shared focus of attention. (Pointing is discussed further on p. 87.)

Learning limits is another opportunity for shared focus of attention, social referencing, and emotional connectedness. When babies crawl toward an electric socket and stop to smile at mommy or daddy, they are signaling their intention. It is a kind of pointing without the finger gesture. This complex, nuanced behavior that includes the baby's memory of the limit, the signal to a parent of their intention, the expectation of being stopped, the knowledge of what will please their parent, and also a wish to please themselves is a creative compromise of conflicting wishes and an amalgamation of a multitude of thoughts and feelings. Once babies get a parent's attention (a kind of social referencing), expecting to be stopped, they accelerate and quickly move toward the socket. These are subtle back and forth communications between parent and baby. There is a merging of external behavior, internal mental processes, and parent-baby communications. The baby's internal world of thoughts and feelings is primed.

When babies' behavior is understood this way, possibilities of responding expand beyond external behavior to include an understanding of their inner experience: "I see, you remember the socket is not for touching. I know you want to touch it. I'm going to help you to stop." Babies' complex thinking about pleasing themselves, pleasing their parents, and learning the limit can be shared and reinforced. Together, they ride on a wave of empathy and love promoting both emotional and behavioral learning.

After numerous repetitions of this kind of parent-child interaction about behavior and its meaning, babies can internalize the limit and make it their own. They will then be able to stop themselves. In time, the impulse to touch the socket will seem to have disappeared. This process is different from obedience. In obedience, behavior is controlled to avoid consequences. In some circumstances, avoiding consequences is a priority. However, most early childhood learning that relates to behavior is also about developing inner mental structures that support behavioral learning. Emotional learning during limit setting reinforces the development of a child's positive sense of self, frustration tolerance, impulse control, value systems of right and wrong, and the capacity for empathy. These inner mental processes are the pillars of behavior.

When understood from the perspective of the child's inner world of thoughts and feelings, children's behavior that seems provocative or disobedient can be understood in terms of conflict and compromise. Behavior that is at first inexplicable becomes understandable; what appears to be a lie may indicate a wish. When an 18-month-old says "No poop," when clearly there is poop in her diaper that needs to be changed, she may be expressing a wish to not have her play interrupted and her poop taken away. When this is recognized, stopping her play and changing diapers can go more smoothly.

Parents and children's attitudes about poop also have an impact on changing diapers and using the potty. Recently a mother told me that her 3-year-old little girl refused to use the potty. "She won't do it because she thinks her poop is disgusting. She says, it stinks, I won't do it." This little girl did something else that her mother thought was disgusting; she picked her nose. I suggested, "Judy might feel that she is disgusting, and she may need to know that her poop smells just the way it is supposed to." The mother looked delighted and pleasurably enticed by my suggestion. The following week the mother reported that after telling her daughter, "Your poop smells just right," to the mother's amazement and to my satisfaction, Judy started using the potty.

I was reminded of something mothers often do to determine if a baby's diaper needs to be changed. They get close to the baby's bottom and take a whiff. For both adults and children, the traverse between pleasure and disgust can be swift: whether it is the smell of poop, nose picking, or making mud pies.

Children's fears that seem irrational become reasonable when understood in a developmental context. A young child who cries inconsolably while getting a haircut may be reacting as if a precious part of his body is being cut off, never to grow back.

Toddlers' clinging to soft cuddly toys and blankets, and frantically protesting their treasured toys being tossed into the swirling, whirling, washing machine that changes their texture and removes their personal scent, can be understood. The treasured teddy bear that soothes all troubles away is not a sign of insecurity; it is a kind of magic that is conjured up and helps to build the child's developing mental structures related to emotion regulation, self-esteem, and frustration tolerance. Attachment to a treasured toy is a developmental achievement. Misunderstanding this can activate parents' ghosts and trigger their anxiety, anger, and frustration.

The imaginary friends that are blamed for writing on walls or the denial of culpability when it is clear may not be the product of a lie but rather may represent an important developmental process. Imaginary friends accused of a child's misbehavior or denial of responsibility may be temporary solutions to the child's efforts to inhibit impulses that are disapproved of by parents. Denying misbehavior may demonstrate the child's beginning self-disapproval for having misbehaved and the growing identification with the parents' disapproval of the behavior. In time the child will develop the psychic structure needed to be able to behave as parents expect. The child is saying, I know it's wrong. I wish I hadn't done it, but I couldn't stop myself. Supporting this developmental process is important: "I know you know it's wrong. I will help you to stop yourself."

Developmentally, these "lies" may be thought of as the emergence of the flexibility and functioning of what has been called narrative truth. In contrast to historical truth, narrative truth is personal. It includes the personal meaning of a past verifiable event. The wish that I didn't do it is a precursor to the ability not to do it. It also lays the foundation to create wish-fulfilling fantasies and at times to achieve them. Integrating the paradox of the value of historical truth, with providing space for narrative truth, is part of mental structure building and the developmental process. The child who says "I didn't do it," when in actuality they did, may be narrating the wish to have not done it before the psychic structure to inhibit the impulse has been developed. Historical truth and narrative truth can co-exist; both continue into adulthood and together enrich our inner worlds.

The repeated dropping or throwing of toys and food that babies and toddlers so frequently do is also a developmental achievement. It is a kind of saying "no." The abilities to let go and to say "no" are important capacities. Their mastery requires much practice.

Understanding babies' and toddlers' inner worlds can help to prevent the intrusion of disturbing ghosts into parent-child interactions. Babies' and young children's external behavior without parents' consideration of its complex underlying meanings can easily be experienced by parents as irrational, provocative, manipulative, mocking, or mean. These interpretations of children's behavior can elicit parental feelings of frustration, anger, helplessness, and inadequacy: feelings that activate challenging ghosts.

The development of internal mental structures is an important goal of early learning: it is a gradual process. Parent-child interactions that include attention to a child's internal world promote complementary behavioral and emotional learning. Learning to use the potty, saying please and thank you, not writing on walls, and not touching electrical sockets are among the easier tasks. Developing frustration tolerance, a moral compass, the capacity for empathy, the ability to love, and a sense of self-worth require a context of safety, empathy, and loving attachments. Babies and young children are highly motivated to please their parents. Loving attachments are needed to promote the development of a rich and functioning inner world.

Ghosts most of the time sleep silently and are nudged only occasionally. Some lay completely dormant until adults become parents. They can pop out, but can also be elusive. When ghosts are triggered by the unacceptable behavior of a child, parents' attention to their own and their child's inner world can be more difficult. This happened to Roberta when Jade was hitting uncontrollably. The next story describes Roberta's insight about Jade's inner world, and her own.

Roberta and Jade
"She won't stop hitting . . ."

It was late September. The pre-nursery playroom and mothers' room had been freshly painted a warm white during summer vacation and the banquette re-upholstered in its familiar pale gray. Glistening new sand filled the opened sandbox. As is customary throughout September of each year, before groups begin in October, two individual visits had been scheduled with each family who had joined a pre-nursery mother-child group. Roberta had only scheduled one: she did not think two warming-up visits were necessary for Jade. "She's 2 years old, she doesn't need two visits."

During Roberta and Jade's visit, Roberta mentioned that Jade had been hitting, but did not elaborate. Their group was meeting the following week and I assumed I would learn more about the hitting then. There were other things Roberta wanted to talk about: learning to swim, sleeping in a bed, and beginning to use the potty filled our half hour visit while Jade played comfortably with the playgroup leaders.

The following week the mothers had all arrived early for the first group of the year. Strollers crowded the waiting alcove and reunion greetings echoed. Through my office door, I heard a loud cry and then quiet. It was 11:00, time to open the playroom. The surroundings were familiar to the children; they had been in programs at the Center since they were a few months old and except for Jade they each had two individual visits before the group began. Three of the children bounded into the playroom and gathered around the sandbox confident that their mothers would remain close. Their mothers sat on the banquette and watched their children from the mothers' room. Two other children entered the playroom more cautiously, holding their mothers' hands. Their mothers helped them to sit at the table and play with puzzles. When the children were comfortable, their mothers joined the others on the banquette. As Roberta entered the playroom, she was reprimanding Jade for hitting one of the children and warning her not to do it again. Jade chose a toy at the far end of the playroom, distant from the other children. Roberta joined the other mothers.

No sooner had we settled on the banquette and begun to talk about developmental changes that had occurred over the summer, than one by one the children came to their mothers either crying because they had been hit by Jade, disturbed by what had happened to another child, or worried about whether they would also be hit. In turn, several of the mothers went into the playroom to get a closer look at what was happening and to protect their children. Playgroup leaders' efforts to help Jade in the playroom had been unsuccessful. The hitting happened so fast and unexpectedly it was difficult to anticipate, or to see what had triggered it.

It was the first group meeting of the year: our pleasure in watching the children play as we talked was replaced with disappointment and anxiety. The mothers were sympathetic to Roberta, but they were also angry. I was concerned.

Jade, who had been an easy-going, well-behaved little girl before the summer, was now hitting everybody, mostly her mother and father, but also the children in playgroup. Not only was this disturbing to her mother, but it was disruptive to the other children and mothers in the group.

Roberta was perplexed by Jade's seemingly unprovoked aggressive behavior and frustrated by her inability to "discipline" her. "I've tried everything: time-outs, no iPad, I even threatened to take her special teddy bear away. I would never really do that. Nothing helps. It's been going on for two weeks. She won't stop hitting."

Jade was a physically sturdy, intelligent little girl. She was tall for her age and competent. She had short, dark hair and was always dressed in blue jeans and a T-shirt. As physically robust, cognitively competent, and socially capable as she had been, her play was now inhibited. Except for hitting, she avoided the other children. This was how Jade looked from the outside.

In order to understand more about Jade's inner world and what might be motivating the hitting, I asked Roberta about Jade's play at home. She mentioned games of hide and seek, chase-and-catch, tickling, and a collection of videos. I asked her to describe some of the details. "Hide and seek is great. I hide behind the door and when Jade enters the room, I jump out at her and shout, 'boo.' She always startles. I played it with my dad." The videos Jade watched included a selection of action stories and fairytales with content often frightening to 2-year-old children. The chase game was primarily played with her father. He ran after Jade and when he caught her, he tickled her while she squealed. Roberta called the game "tickle-torture."

The following elements of Roberta's description of their play captured my attention: "She always startles, I played it with my dad, and 'tickle-torture.'" Since a startle is a noticeable indication of disequilibrium, "tickle-torture" alludes to pain, and "I played it with my dad" suggested that ghosts had arrived, I commented, "These sound like high arousal games which are important, but sometimes scare little children and need to be modified to the right intensity." Roberta disagreed and contradicted me, "Jade never gets scared." I remarked, "Really? Never?"

Roberta's memories of her own father when she was a little girl flooded out. She told us, almost bragging, "My father wanted a son. He taught me to be tough like he was, not scared like my mother. He taught me to do scary things like climb trees and ride my bike down a steep hill with no hands. We always watched horror movies together. At the amusement park near our house, we went on the big roller coaster and sneaked around the haunted house, avoiding the moving skeletons and booby traps. My dad always got me past the ticket collectors because he lied about my age. I guess I was a tomboy."

In the midst of Roberta's carnival memories, I was reminded of the crackles on the smooth surface of a juicy candy apple that can cut your tongue: the pain beneath the sweet surface. I said, "It seems like appearing not scared and sharing frightening experiences with your father helped you to feel loved and accepted by him. I wonder whether Jade might be feeling some of the same things." This was a new way for Roberta to think about her memories, but it seemed to strike a chord. Perhaps recounting her memories triggered remnants of scared feelings. I continued, "Sometimes children hit when they are frightened. Discipline won't help them to stop hitting if they're scared. Acknowledging scared feelings, feeling protected, and safe might."

The following week, as we began to consider the activities and situations that might be frightening to Jade, a distant memory of Roberta's began to emerge. At first the memory was vague and then increasingly distinct. Her memory of a small music-box with a twirling ballerina and a lilting melody began to surface and frequently come to mind. Roberta longingly tried to recall the name and melody of the music-box lullaby. When she was a little girl the music-box was kept on a high shelf in her bedroom: it was rarely taken down. It was fragile and delicate, the opposite of brave and tough. At the same time this memory was coming into focus, Roberta began to recognize moments when Jade was scared. She began to limit the frightening videos and modified the scary games. She also began to help Jade talk about her scary feelings. The distant melody of "Fur Elise" and the twirling ballerina were now shining bright. By the next week, the hitting had stopped. The joy returned to the playroom and the warm support among the mothers was restored. The music-box memory that had remained in the shadows emerged with all its delicate details. It represented the little girl who had frightening feelings that Roberta had needed to keep far away, on a high shelf, out of reach.

Roberta had not thought about her play with her father for many years. She had never thought about the music-box. There was much to understand about her relationship with her father and his attitudes about gender. There was also more for Roberta to understand about herself, her feelings about being a woman, and having a daughter.

Cultural beliefs, shared fantasies, and superstitions among groups of people are also part of the inner world of individuals: for example, the Tooth Fairy, Santa, and Friday the 13th. Holidays like Thanksgiving, Hanukkah, and Christmas are part of our collective inner worlds. Catastrophic events like tsunamis, earthquakes, fires, plane crashes, and school shootings have an impact on large numbers of people, and affect our combined inner worlds. Terrorist attacks also have this impact.

Our collective inner worlds were shaken on September 11, 2001, the day the Twin Towers were attacked in New York City. It is remembered in specific ways by New Yorkers. For many, any severe, clear, blue sky triggers flashes of 9/11 anxieties. Memories are vivid of the planes flying low over the city as if in slow motion moments before hitting the towers. The thick scent of burning debris and flesh that filled the air is indelible. The images repeatedly broadcast of the towers being hit and crumbling to the ground are easily recalled. For me, the most intense part of my memory is the throng of dazed, silent people walking slowly up Madison Avenue; their clothes covered with white soot, their faces smeared by tears mixed with ashes, and vacant eyes.

When parent-child groups resumed in October, all the women shared a concern that was conveyed in the following question, "How do I help my child feel safe when I no longer feel safe?" I reframed their question about an event that was unfamiliar and frightening, the terrorist attack on NYC, into one that was known. I responded, "You were faced with this dilemma before September 11th, but in a different way." I told them that their question restated is, "How do I help my child feel safe as he learns about the universality and inevitability of death?" The women were able to shift their perspective from confronting a new terror to re-experiencing a more or less mastered fact of life. The details of each mother's own ideas about death and teaching children about death were discussed. Past trauma and current anxieties related to death and talking to children about death were also explored.

The women then went on to create memory narratives about September 11th with their children. Their narratives varied depending on the age of their children, proximity to the Twin Towers, the parents' immediate reaction of terror, whether they knew anyone who had died in the attacks, and their recovery in the days and weeks following. Children's exposure to televised images, news reports, and adult reactions were considered. Narratives included, "Mommy and daddy are taking care of you even when bad things are happening. We are all safe now." In time they added, "That was last week, that was last month, and then, you are remembering something that happened a long time ago."

4 Parents' Insights

Parents' insights about their childhood memories and the underlying meanings of their own and their children's behavior are transformative ingredients of the magic between parents and young children. Insight, a new perspective and deepening more complex understanding of themselves and their children, has intellectual and emotional components; both are needed. As illustrated throughout these stories, parents' strong emotions are sparked while interacting with their children. These feelings trigger repetitions of their own childhood relationships. Ghosts are activated. Emerging memories provide clues to understanding the impact of the ghosts. Specific elements of childhood memories have symbolic meaning that can be interpreted. Some elements of memories have unconscious meaning. The surface content disguises the underlying meaning. Understanding both the conscious and unconscious meanings of memories that are linked to current parent-child interactions and childrearing approaches can transform angry interactions into understanding, bewilderment into clarity, and memory enactments into insight.

In the following vignette, Claudia's insight about the meaning of a particular sexual memory was transformative. Claudia, a mothers' group member, had a vivid, persistent, yet illogical recurring memory since she was a little girl. In the middle of an excited mothers' group discussion about parents' sex lives when they have young children, Claudia recounted a memory that at first seemed out of context. "When I was about 8 years old, I was alone in the kitchen and there was a knock on the screen door. I approached the door and saw an Easter Bunny. He was standing on two legs, much taller than I was, holding a brown basket with two brightly colored eggs in a nest of brown grass. I know this sounds impossible, but my memory is clear, it feels like it actually happened. I ran upstairs to my parents who were still in bed and told them about this amazing thing that I saw." The women in the group offered possible rational explanations. "A grown-up may have been dressed in a bunny costume. It could have been a toy bunny." Claudia insisted, "It was real, it was alive, I know it sounds impossible, but I remember it clearly." Claudia had repeated this memory to others many times and was always told, "It never happened." Being told it never happened, and also believing herself that it sounded unrealistic, had never changed her feelings about the memory or the meaning it had for her.

At this moment, Claudia became contemplative. Her distant gaze seemed inner focused, she remained still – all indications of self-reflection. Our lively group discussion continued about whether parents lock the bedroom door when they have sex, have sex when sharing a room with their children, or when the children are sleeping in their bed with them. Bright-eyed and energized, Claudia chimed in, "This never occurred to me before. My parents always told me that I once walked in on them when they were having sex, but I never remembered it. Maybe the unrealistic Easter Bunny was my way of remembering the unimaginable, incomprehensible sight of my parents having sex."

The excitement Claudia felt and her new perspective during our discussion about parental sex had triggered the memory. Her experience being a mother with young children created a new context and the new meaning that she attributed to her memory. The meaning of her memory had dramatically changed. Specific images in Claudia's memory supported her sexual interpretation of her memory: two brightly colored eggs, the brown grass, her parents in bed, and the size of the bunny that placed his genitals at Claudia's eye level.

Claudia's fanciful memory of an Easter Bunny that had seemed real to her was accompanied with a memory narrative but the event the memory represented to Claudia, seeing her parents having sex, had not been known or processed. It had remained disguised in her memory by the fantastic Easter Bunny. Furthermore, it was being enacted when she and her husband were having sex and their bedroom door was left open to their children. Until Claudia's moment of insight about the content of her memory and her feelings, re-living in action had replaced remembering. As the meaning of her memory changed, the clarity of the image of the Easter Bunny, the basket and eggs, and especially the telling her parents in bed about the bunny began to fade. Claudia's Easter Bunny memory is also an example of the inability of young children to understand adult sex, or to process it. Claudia and her husband began to close their door while they were having sex.

In the next story, Claire's revived memory of a kiss and her insight about its meaning became a useful warning.

Claire and Beverly "My memory of a kiss . . ."

Claire was an attractive woman in her early forties. Her husband was a physician. They had three children: a 14-year-old daughter, 8-year-old son, and Beverly, a 3-year-old little girl with whom Claire was in a mother-child group. Claire had been a practicing attorney in a small law firm until her second child was born. She had a busy home, with beginning teenage sexual excitement that set the stage for the emergence of her childhood sexual memories.

The mothers' group that Claire was in had been meeting for over two years. The women in the group had shared many intimate details about their children, themselves, and their marriages. It was an unusually hot day in May and I had decided to serve iced coffee to the mothers. The children were huddled around a large basin of water, cooling their hands and arms up to their elbows. The mothers and I had just settled on the banquette when Claire mentioned a recent newspaper article that described the sexual abuse of a young girl. Claire declared her intention to teach Beverly, now 3 years old, how to protect herself. She wanted to ensure that Beverly would never be sexually abused. I wondered to myself about her focus on Beverly and the omission of any reference to her 14-year-old daughter or 8-year-old son in this context.

Claire described how she was warning Beverly about potential dangers and teaching self-protective strategies to her. "Never talk to strangers, never take candy from strangers, never get into a car with strangers." I could imagine how frightening these warnings might be to a 3-year-old and how unsafe and unprotected it could make Beverly feel. In addition, I wondered why Claire was warning Beverly about strangers since 3-year-old children are rarely alone with strangers and the parents of a sexually abused child often know the abuser.

While the newspaper story was disturbing, I wondered what personal experiences Claire had that might be related to it. In the middle of enumerating her instructions to Beverly and appearing startled, Claire remembered a kiss when she was 14 years old. Her father's friend put his hands on her bottom and kissed her in a way that tickled the inner edge of her lips with his tongue. She never told her parents, or anyone, and had not thought about it for many years.

Claire's older daughter was now 14 years old, the same age Claire had been when kissed and touched. And while Claire thought the newspaper story had triggered her concern, her daughter being the same age as she was when inappropriately touched and kissed may have created the personal context for her emerging memory and worry.

From Claire's description of the kiss, I wondered about the sexual shame, guilt, and arousal Claire might have felt when her father's friend kissed her, and whether any of these feelings motivated her to keep the kiss secret. I also wondered whether as a child, Claire felt unprotected in other ways that might have contributed to not telling her parents about the kiss. With both Claire and Beverly in mind, I said, "It is parents' responsibility to protect their children. Little children cannot protect themselves. I wonder when you felt unprotected." Claire then told the group, "When I was 10 years old, my little brother who was 8 always spied on me when I was in the bathroom. When I told my parents, they accused me of teasing him and said that I liked the attention."

I wondered whether Claire's memory about her parents' accusations and disdain in response to her "teasing" her brother also applied to the kiss and contributed to her anxiety about Beverly being sexually abused. I stayed with another comment about Claire's safety and added her memory about her parents' disapproval of her teasing. "Not only do you remember your parents not protecting you, but in addition you remember them blaming you for your brother's peeping and criticizing you for any excitement or pleasure you got from it." Claire repeated, "I never told my parents about the kiss." I took Claire's statement as a confirmation that in some ways she thought the kiss was her fault and she felt ashamed. I continued, "Maybe you also thought it was your fault that your father's friend kissed you with his tongue and touched you on your bottom. Maybe it is part of the reason for not telling your parents." The room was quiet. I added, "Little children cannot protect themselves. They learn to protect themselves when they feel protected by their parents. In addition, when their body pleasures are recognized, they learn when and with whom pleasurable touching and kissing are ok, and when and with whom they are not."

In order to discuss with the mothers the ways in which parents can lay the foundation for young children to protect themselves when they are older, I asked, "What are some of the body pleasures the children are learning about now? Which are ok with you, and which are not? And, what are some of the different ways in which the children are currently trying to avoid being touched by family members, and by others? When do they say no to kisses or handshakes: or recoil when a stranger touches them? When do you support them and say, 'I see you didn't like it when the man in the elevator touched you?' When do you require them to be touched in ways they don't want? For example, being examined by the doctor. And when do you coerce them to be touched or bribe them with treats? When are they asked to be nice and kiss someone so as not to hurt their feelings?" In these ways, I confronted the mothers in order to make my point clear. I added, "When do you support your children to say no?" The allusions to child sexual abuse scenarios in my questions about what happens between parents and young children were obvious, as was the implied protection of both being entitled and empowered to say no, and entitled to have body pleasures in safe, acceptable ways. A rich discussion followed. The women appreciated the potential importance of supporting both body pleasure and saying no.

The following week, Claire told the group that she had decided to discontinue the male babysitter in his twenties she had hired recently and with whom she did not feel "quite comfortable." It was not clear whether Claire's discomfort was in response to the babysitter's gender, age, or behavior. The babysitter was a surprise to us. The women believed that the babysitter also might have posed a threat to Claire's 14-year-old daughter. This had not occurred to Claire. She had denied what was a glaring possibility to the other mothers.

Claire now recognized that a 3-year-old is not able to protect herself. She also understood that in certain situations, the best way to teach Beverly now and lay the foundation for the future was to support her when she said no to being touched. When Beverly protested, but needed to be touched, for example by the doctor or when getting her nails cut, Claire recognized the importance of acknowledging and accepting her feelings, and supporting communications about them. Beverly was no longer required to do high-fives with their neighbor, sit on her uncle's lap whom she saw only on occasion, or be kissed when she did not want to be. In some ways, Claire realized that while she had been hyper-vigilant about teaching Beverly to protect herself, at the same time she was denying her own protective and supportive role. She also recognized that she did not feel protected by her own parents when she was inappropriately kissed and touched by their friend, and furthermore did not feel safe enough to tell them.

Claire became more accepting of the normal body pleasures children enjoy. In addition, Claire began to address her reactions to her teenage daughter's developing sexuality and the revival of her own teenage sexual memories. Claire stopped bathing Beverly with her 8-year-old brother. She now believed that bathing her children together had been linked to her memories about her brother peeping at her in the bathroom when she was a little girl and her parents' accusations. Claire's childhood memories now had new meaning. Her feelings about her brother spying on her now included both her excitement and not liking it. The memory of her parents' accusations and the shame she felt had shifted. She was now more accepting of both kinds of feelings. Claire's insight about her childhood memories enabled her to protect her children better.

Parents have both loving and protective ghosts, and rejecting and frightening ghosts. Both are needed to organize the inner world of memories, thoughts, and feelings. Without memories that contain both kinds of ghosts, there can be internal chaos or emptiness. Parents have had childhoods that included both emotionally painful and pleasurable emotions. Children experience safety and terror, care and neglect, love and disapproval: if not in actuality, in fantasy. Parents' memories may trigger unintended angry, frightening, rejecting, or neglectful interactions with their young children, and sometimes feelings of helplessness. Exploring memories can feel dangerous. Feelings of safety are needed to confront ghosts and acquire insight. Understanding memories is empowering.

Parents being screamed at by their children can trigger memories of being yelled at by their own parents. Even babies crying can be experienced by their parents as painful disapproval or criticism. These ghosts can be particularly haunting and influence parents' responses to their crying babies.

Many years ago, a mother told me that when her baby was alone in his room and began to cry, she thought he was angry with her. She confessed, "In a way, I feel like he's calling me a bad mommy. I don't know if I should go to him." I responded, "I wonder if you are remembering your mommy yelling at you and calling you a bad little girl." She remained thoughtful. Appearing self-reflective and perhaps a little sad, indicating a shift in her inner state, I added, "I imagine your baby is crying because he misses you and wants you to hold him." This idea about her baby wanting to be close to her opened up a stream of memories about being neglected by her mother. Before this moment, they had been too painful to voice. Insight about her memories was now possible.

Sibling rivalry among young children can trigger parents' disturbing memories. Recently, a mother told me a memory about her older brother hitting and teasing her when they were young children. "He took my special doll and threatened to throw it out the window. He hit me and twisted my arm. My parents refused to help me. They wanted me to be strong and independent." Now a mother, she was distraught about the endless physical fighting between her 2-year-old twins. "They punch and kick each other. There's nothing I can do. I guess it's just boys being boys." I connected her memory about her brother teasing and hurting her, with what seemed to be her current belief that it was ok for siblings to hurt each other. I related her memory about her parents refusing to protect her from her brother, with her current feelings of helplessness with her own children. Becoming aware that she was re-living her childhood helplessness, inability to get help from her parents, and belief that boys are inherently hurtful enabled her to intervene with her sons and prevent them from hurting each other.

Parents' predictions about their babies are derived from their inner worlds of thoughts, feelings, and memories, and have an impact on their children. Jonah was 3 years old when his mother consulted with me. Performing roles was his exclusive kind of play. His mother was concerned that his only play was to put on shows and enact a variety of roles for her. There were no stories to his performances, only different roles with costumes and props. The most important part of Jonah's pretend play was that his mother be his audience. She was concerned about the limited range of his play and wondered why performing for her was his play preference. She said, "There is something about his play that's not right, he only plays different roles and wants me to be the audience." I wondered what his mother was reacting to and how Jonah's role-playing might be different from typical, adaptive role-play, and what it was triggering in his mother.

In the midst of our trying to understand the meaning of Jonah's performing and what it meant to his mother she commented, "Since the moment he was born, I thought he was gay. What was I thinking? He was a newborn. Why was I thinking that? Why do I still think that?" We did not answer these questions, but her surprise at her own thinking and for the first time questioning the origins of her belief that Jonah was gay was followed by a change in his play. Jonah began playing a variety of other games. His performing for his mother markedly diminished. His mother's conviction that he was gay began to fade. Her awareness that the origins of her idea that Jonah was gay did not seem to have anything to do with Jonah had changed something between them even though we could not identify what it was. Perhaps Jonah no longer needed to play a role because he felt seen by his mother in a new way. The important part of this story is not whether Jonah was gay, or would be gay when he grew up. What is interesting about this vignette is that for the first time, Jonah's mother questioned her own thinking about Jonah. Her insight was about the onset of her belief when Jonah was a newborn. The meaning of her belief had changed from a prediction to a fantasy that she was interested in understanding.

A parent's emerging fear can herald renewed working-through of unresolved past events. Kari joined a mother-baby group with Carson and Cassandra, who were 10 months old. When they turned 1 year old, Kari developed a fear that they would be kidnapped. When she saw a car drive slowly past their suburban home, she felt convinced of the danger; although she believed it probably was not true. When the children were in the garden and Kari saw the car drive past her house several times, she became panicky.

Kari had been adopted when she was an infant and grew up being told that her adoption had become final when she was 1 year old, the same age her twins would soon be. She believed, "Being adopted was never an issue for me. I have the best parents." When I asked her more about the car that drove past her house, she remarked, "A woman was driving." I asked her who she thought the woman might be. She spontaneously blurted out the first thing that popped into her mind, "Maybe it's my biological mother." Kari's idea, and her attempt to make a joke, opened up the exploration of her thoughts and feelings about having been adopted that had been triggered by having given birth to Carson and Cassandra, the first people she ever knew who were genetically related to her, and by her ability to do something that had been important to her mother but that she had been unable to do.

Children's temper tantrums can be disturbing. They can include screaming, kicking, head banging, and hitting. Because of the intensity of feelings they display as well as evoke in parents, they are fertile ground for ghosts. During a child's first 3 years of life, the specifics of many parents' evoked feelings signal the re-emergence of childhood memories. These revivals may be conscious or unconscious. Miranda and her 3-year-old son, Keith, were in a mother-child group. Miranda told us about Keith's raging temper tantrums with the slightest provocation. "His meltdowns have gotten worse. I know it's normal, but I can't stand it." The latest one was triggered when Keith's older brother had returned home from a birthday party with a pack of bubble gum. He gave one piece to Keith, but Keith wanted the entire pack. Keith began crying and in a vicious rage shouted, "I hate you. You don't love me."

Miranda continued to describe how lately even slight frustrations triggered Keith's temper tantrums. She also described her own helplessness and harsh anger in response. She said, "I yell at him and threaten punishments, which I know I'm never going to follow through with. Keith looks so scared. I'm so mean to him. I call him names, I say things like, you are a bad boy and nobody will like you." I asked Miranda to tell us more about her own helplessness and what was making her so angry.

Miranda had an insight as she shifted her focus from Keith to herself. She realized that at the core of her angry, helpless reactions to her son were her own childhood memories filled with despairing pain of feeling unloved, misunderstood, and blamed. Vivid memories of her brother's tantrums and her mother's frightening screams were revived. Her son's behavior had triggered her own, mostly successfully warded off, painful feelings and her mother's terrifying rage at a time when Miranda was vulnerable and helpless. With this insight she was able to respond to Keith with comfort and support, rather than being angry and punitive. She recognized and accepted his feelings, and communicated her understanding clearly to him. For example, the next time Keith had a temper tantrum she said, "I agree it's not fair. You got one lollipop and you wanted more." Feeling understood helped Keith to re-regulate more quickly and also decreased the frequency of his tantrums.

Painful childhood memories can evoke reactive, compensatory responses that on the surface are the opposite of the memories, but result in related difficulties. In the next story, Naomi's startling insight about breastfeeding changed many aspects of her interactions with her 17-month-old son, Wally, as well as with her husband.

Naomi and Wally
"Breastfeeding is more than I ever imagined . . ."

When Naomi was 10 years old, as she sat eating breakfast, her mother jumped up from the table to answer the phone, tripped, and spilled a cup of scalding coffee on Naomi. The coffee blistered her face, shoulders, and thighs. The accident was horrendous and the treatments painful. By the time Naomi was 12 years old her face was completely healed. One small scar remained on her thigh. For Naomi, worse than the accident and the treatments was the hostile fury she experienced as a child and continued to experience from her mother. Perhaps in some ways for Naomi the two experiences, the blistering hot coffee and her mother's anger, were merged. Throughout her teen years, following her mother's "explosive rages" and her father's absence, Naomi lay on her bed soothing herself by counting the years remaining till she would grow up and leave home, marry, and have a baby. The idealized mother-baby relationship she envisioned was the remedy for her emotional pain. Naomi had told this story to me when she joined the mother-toddler group with her 17-month-old son, Wally.

It was mid-November and raining heavily. Wet coats and stroller-covers draped the waiting room chairs and dripped onto the floor, creating little puddles. Rain boots were removed and left to dry. The children's joy was not dampened by the weather. The playroom carpet was scattered with toys. The familiar busy hum filled the room. The mothers and I were beginning to know each other. It was the fifth time the group was meeting. We had talked about their pregnancies, labor and deliveries, and how each child's name was chosen. A feeling of safety had been created. We had begun to talk about the ways in which each mother wanted to be like her own mother and the ways she wanted to be different. We had started to talk about how specific childhood memories were related to current interactions with their children.

The children were exploring the playroom, occasionally touching base with their mothers. Wally sat on his mother's lap; his face nuzzled into her breasts. At this moment, brimming with conflict, Naomi told us, "I'm still breastfeeding, but not sure if I want to continue. Many people think Wally's too old to nurse. He's now 17 months, but I think I'm giving him all the attention, love, and security he needs. He's completely safe. I'm giving him all the things I never had when I was a child." Naomi's childhood memories about her accident, loneliness, and unhappiness had been triggered; she described her current feelings of anxiety and insecurity. Ghosts were hovering. Weaning from breastfeeding occurs at different ages, for different reasons. What was important for Naomi was to understand her conflict about whether to continue to nurse or not.

Naomi went on to describe her relationship with Wally as "blissfully happy." However, in addition to her authentic statements of deep love for Wally, her profound pleasures and rewards being a mother – specifically her satisfactions with breastfeeding – were intermittent, brief asides that conveyed her underlying frustration, resentment, and anxiety. She gingerly alluded to the unrelenting demands of caring for a toddler. "My husband doesn't do any childcare. He never changed a diaper. I feel like a single mom. I do it all. I fall into bed exhausted at 8:00."

Naomi's description of her husband reminded me about her description of her father's absence when she was a child and her mother screamed at her. She had needed her father's help, but did not get it. I wondered if this was being repeated with her husband. "I fall into bed exhausted" reminded me of her childhood memory of lying on her bed, envisioning an idealized reparative version of becoming a mother, and how different the actuality is.

Naomi emphasized her exclusive care of Wally. "I never use a babysitter. My parents don't help at all and I wouldn't want them to. I'm with Wally all the time. I never do anything else. I never see my friends or even talk to them on the phone. I even sleep with Wally. Wally nurses all day and all night. I love breastfeeding. We are very close." Naomi added, "I'm quick to get angry at other people, but I never get angry at Wally. The other day I was so angry yelling at the super in my building. I worry about how my anger at other people will affect Wally."

Naomi had talked about how close she and Wally were, all the love, comfort, and security she was providing for him, and how gratified she was by their relationship. Simultaneously, she had conveyed that she was stressed, resentful, and angry. She denied being angry with Wally, but worried about her anger at others. She had described some elements that were preventing her from making a decision about continuing to breastfeed or to wean, but remained stuck in her conflict. There was more to understand.

In order to understand more, I asked Naomi what she thought about while she was nursing. Naomi described breastfeeding as a pleasurable time to think about things other than Wally. "I think about things I need to do, friends to call, sometimes I read, I send emails, things like that. I know he's safe and happy, I can think about other things." I summarized what Naomi had been saying. "It sounds like breastfeeding is very satisfying for you. While breastfeeding you can feel close to Wally, feel like you are giving him all the love and security he needs, and at the same time you can think about other things." Naomi nodded and I continued, "You don't need to talk to him, look at him, worry about him, or play with him." Naomi cautiously smiled in agreement with my slight twist on her words. Feeling encouraged that new meanings were emerging for Naomi, I went on, "It sounds like the only time you get away from Wally is while you are breastfeeding." Without skipping a beat, Naomi responded, "The only break I get is when I'm breastfeeding. I'm with him all the time. I never leave him with anyone. Breastfeeding is the only break I get." A new meaning of breastfeeding crystalized for Naomi.

The following week, Naomi told us that she had begun to wean Wally. She stated, "I realized that nursing is my way of getting away from Wally." My comment to Naomi the prior week, "It sounds like the only time you get away from Wally is while you are breastfeeding," hit a nerve that could have been painful, but instead felt true in a way that enabled Naomi to face an aspect of her internal conflict between continuing to nurse or stopping, of which she had been unaware.

During the next several weeks we talked in the mothers' group about the different ways in which children experience love and security at each phase of development. We also talked about ways, other than nursing, in which the mother-baby relationship is unique. In addition, we talked about the typical anxieties mothers feel about their toddlers' safety.

Naomi and Wally began to discover multiple pleasurable ways of being together. Naomi began to recognize the unique aspects of her relationship with Wally in addition to breastfeeding. Gradually, she arranged for a babysitter a few hours a week and helped Wally to sleep in his crib. Wally and his father began to spend more time together. Baths, reading, and block building became some of their favorite activities. Gradually and easily for both Wally and Naomi, by the time Wally was 20 months old, he was no longer nursing.

Naomi's painful childhood memories about her accident, her mother's hostile and disapproving angry rages, her father's absence, her feelings of anger, loneliness, and insecurity that were eased by breastfeeding, and her teenage fantasies of getting away from her parents had all been activated and had influenced her interactions with Wally. Naomi now recognized that her childhood memories had been motivating many of her interactions, not only with Wally, but also with her husband.

Naomi realized that any separation from Wally had felt like she was abandoning him, any childcare help had felt like she was neglecting him, any time Wally was with his father had felt like she was ignoring him, and weaning had seemed like she was rejecting him. In addition, for Naomi, breastfeeding had retained a magical meaning of protection that would keep Wally safe. Elements of Naomi's childhood memories had invaded her interactions with Wally. Naomi's insights and the emotional shifts they encompassed enabled her to better meet Wally's changing developmental needs and her own.

In the next story, acquiring insight was more complicated because the connections between childhood memories and current life events were entangled, obscured, and difficult to understand. The feelings were warded off.

Darcy and Millie
"She's just a baby . . ."

Millie was a cheerful, socially engaging 22-month-old little girl with two mothers; she was in a mother-child group with her mother Darcy. Millie participated joyfully in all play activities. Her language was well developed for her age. She was beginning to establish relationships with the other children in the group. Turn taking was easy for her and her shared fun in joint activities with other children was apparent. Millie looked mature for her age with long, dark wavy hair and thick bangs. She frequently wore a pretty smocked dress.

Millie did not touch base with her mother during the group, but quickly began turning to the playgroup leaders who were supervising the children. Millie initiated interactions with the playgroup leaders in order to process events that had occurred, to share the pleasure of her play, and to get help when needed. Her social referencing with playgroup leaders, her verbal and nonverbal communications about her thoughts and feelings, were clear. They included initiating shared smiles while delighting in the pleasure of completing a puzzle or block construction. When a child tried to take a toy away from her, she asserted, "My turn," held on tight, and looked to a playgroup leader signaling what was happening, or that she wanted support, or needed help. She focused her attention on playgroup leaders when they created narratives about events. For example, "It's your turn. Laura needs to wait. I'm going to help her." Millie was thriving.

Millie's mother Darcy was an active participant in the mothers' group that had been meeting weekly since October. It was now mid-November. Darcy's view of Millie was markedly different than mine. Darcy frequently commented, "She's just a happy baby. She doesn't understand anything. I don't think she has any thoughts or feelings yet, she's only 22 months old." It seemed as though Darcy needed to deny Millie's inner world: her developing mind.

Millie's other mother did not participate in the group and Darcy rarely talked about her. She was a lawyer at a large firm that Darcy had also worked at before maternity leave. I had never met her and knew little about their relationship or her relationship with Millie. Darcy had given birth to Millie and primarily took care of her.

When a child's inner world is unacknowledged by her mother, as Millie's was by Darcy, and the motivation to deny it is strong, the depth of their relationship and the pleasure for each is limited. Darcy maintained her view, "Millie is just a baby. She doesn't really know me. She doesn't understand anything." I wondered about the childhood memories contributing to Darcy's ideas about Millie's developing mind, how Millie having two mothers influenced Darcy's insistence that "She's just a baby," and what Millie's other mother thought about Millie's inner world.

During the sixth week we were meeting, another little girl in the playgroup grabbed a doll from Millie. Looking stunned, Millie signaled a need for help to a playgroup leader who put into words what had occurred. "Heidi grabbed the doll from you, you didn't like that, let's tell her it's your turn and you want it back." She said to Heidi, "You wanted the doll, but it's Millie's turn now. I'm going to help you to give it back to Millie and find something else for you to play." A few moments later Millie grabbed a puzzle away from Heidi. The playgroup leader then said, "Millie, do you know what I think happened? You grabbed from Heidi just like Heidi grabbed from you." Millie then handed the puzzle back to Heidi and continued to play with the doll. For Millie, grabbing the puzzle seemed to be a way for her to process again with the playgroup leader what had happened when Heidi had grabbed the doll with which she had been playing, how she and Heidi felt, and to integrate that the "no grabbing" rule is for everyone. She was learning that complex social interactions and feelings could be talked about and understood.

At the same time these interactions were occurring among the children and the playgroup leaders, Darcy was describing Millie: "I don't think she's that aware, she's just a baby. I'm going away next month; she won't even notice." I commented, "It seems hard for you to imagine that Millie notices or cares about anything, including you." Darcy looked reflective, but did not say anything. I wondered whether Darcy also believed that Millie didn't notice that she had two mommies. Nothing more was said. After the group in front of her mother, Millie grabbed a cookie from Heidi. Heidi cried; Darcy giggled and ignored what had occurred. Millie ate the cookie. I was surprised by Darcy's response; Heidi's mother was angry.

During our next group meeting, when the other women were describing their children's typical 2-year-old oppositional behavior, Darcy restated, but this time somewhat differently, "Millie's just a baby. She never opposes me. She always does what I want her to do. She always wants what I want. She never has her own thoughts or feelings."

Darcy's statement indicated an internal shift had occurred and provided a new understanding of her belief about Millie being "just a baby." I said, "Being just a baby seems to mean Millie is at one with you and shares all the same thoughts and feelings that you have." Darcy remained quiet. I described the sequence of grabbing among the children that had occurred the week before. Then I added, "I wonder whether Millie grabbed the cookie from Heidi in front of you because she wanted to know what you thought about it." Darcy now seemed pleased with the possibility that Millie cared about her thoughts. She became quietly introspective. The idea that she and Millie could have different thoughts and feelings, that Millie wanted to know her mother's thoughts and feelings, and that she could be influenced by her mother's thoughts was dawning on Darcy and seemed to interest her.

A turning point occurred the following week when Darcy began to preface statements that denied Millie's inner world with the phrase, "I wonder why I think . . . ?" This was a major shift. I understood this significant change to represent Darcy's emerging interest in the meaning of her idea that Millie was unaware of everything, had no thoughts and feelings of her own, and was "just a baby." It also demonstrated that Darcy was thinking about thinking; she was reflecting on her own thoughts. Insight was now possible.

Two weeks later Darcy began with, "I don't know why I think Millie doesn't know anything or think about anything. Why do I think she's just a baby?" I responded, "That is an important question. Who was the baby in your family?" Darcy continued with what I thought was a non sequitur: "My self-esteem is from my dad. He always said that I could do anything, be anything, and have anything. My mother always said that I couldn't do anything. What I wanted didn't count. I was too young for everything. I was just dismissed." I responded, "Maybe your mother saw you as just a baby."

The following week, Darcy told us that her view had changed. "Millie knows more than I had thought. She needs me to tell her more about what's happening and what I think. She also has her own thoughts." Darcy now believed that Millie might miss her while she was away on vacation and planned to FaceTime with her.

Several things contributed to Darcy's insight. First, Millie developed a trusting, supportive relationship with the playgroup leaders who responded to her social referencing and helped her to seek direct contact with her mother when she needed to feel connected with her for reassurance, shared pleasure, information, or validation. When Millie approached her mother, I said things like, "Millie wants to show you what she did, or Millie wants to know what you think about Heidi grabbing the doll." This helped to demonstrate to Darcy that Millie did care about what she thought and how she felt. Perhaps more importantly, it helped Darcy and Millie to feel more emotionally connected. Second, the conviction of the other mothers in the group that their children were aware – that they think, feel, know, and have intentions – increased Darcy's self-questioning about her denial of Millie's thoughts and feelings. Third, my description that the grabbing sequence among the children was motivated by wishes and feelings and evoked reactions increased Darcy's awareness that not only did Millie have complex thoughts and feelings, but also that she cared and needed to know what her mother thought and felt. Perhaps most important, Darcy began to question her denial of Millie's inner world. She connected her memories about her own mother devaluing and dismissing her abilities, feelings, and wishes to her conviction that Millie was "just a baby." She realized now that she was treating Millie the way she remembered her mother had treated her. This insight had changed Darcy's interactions with Millie. Another important theme remained.

The ways in which Darcy's view of Millie as "just a baby" had been related to Darcy's thoughts and feelings about Millie having two mothers had not yet been explored. If Millie was "just a baby," Darcy could more easily defer thinking about and talking to Millie about what it meant to have two mothers. Darcy's new understanding that she could influence what Millie thought about having two mothers made thinking and talking about it possible. Darcy began to talk in the mothers' group about Millie's developing awareness of different kinds of families.

5 Being a Parent

When women become mothers and men become fathers they are catapulted into new pleasures and new stresses. The merry-go-round of feelings turns quickly. Childhood memories explode. There is exhilaration, anxiety, and uncertainty; most of all, there is change. Childhood memories are activated in a new and powerful context – the parent-child love relationship. The intensity of the feelings aroused in interaction with babies and young children provides a unique opportunity for parents to gain personal insight.

Mother-father-baby is the most frequently depicted family constellation. It has also been the most studied. However, there are multiple variations. Single parents, same-sex parents, and transgender parent families are increasingly being established and are receiving more attention. Research to date suggests that differing family configurations have more in common than not in terms of psychodynamics and outcomes. In one of my mother-baby groups many years ago there were five women married to men, and one single mother. There were aspects of being single that the married women envied and elements of being married that the single mother envied. Darcy in the prior story had a wife and a daughter, Millie. Millie had two mothers. Discussions in both of these groups expanded everyone's thinking about family.

There are exciting shared couple parts to becoming parents and personal ones. There are fluctuating, fleeting imaginings. Visions of the future and memories of the past collide. They are played with, rejected, owned, and revised. Parents think about how they want to be the same as and in what ways different from their own parents. The parent yearned for emerges. Some elements of this process are silent and internal; others surface and are shared. A single parent's and a couple's decision to have a child occur in the context of the personal meaning it has for each.

For all parents, there are shifts in roles and identities. Like quick-silver they shimmer, wobble, and rapidly change shape. For couples, role and identity transitions of each have an impact on the other, and on their relationship. Sometimes the process of change in one is out of sync with changes in the other. Parenting styles and childrearing ideas may be complementary or disturbingly different. Watching a romantic sexual partner in a parent role can be pleasing or unsettling. These shifting internal landscapes and their external impact are occurring in the context of the pleasures and stresses of caring for babies and young children. Both the gratifications and the tensions are enormous. Childhood memories sprout and take root. Ghosts begin to stir.

There are unique aspects to becoming a mother and to becoming a father that are specific to being a woman or being a man. From the moment an adolescent girl gets her first period and a boy first ejaculates, they have physical evidence of their potential fertility. The idea of becoming a mother or a father is substantiated bodily for both. However, the biological and the cultural meaning differences are significant.

When girls begin to menstruate, the blood, the inconvenience, and the cramps accompany the pride and centrality of the possibility of motherhood. The congratulations and warnings emphasize the fertility meaning of menstruation. For boys, the pleasure of orgasm is primary. The fertility meaning is secondary, invoked as a cautionary note to pursuing sexual pleasure. These differences of becoming a man and becoming a woman may be at the core of differing emotional reactions to becoming a mother and becoming a father.

In addition to gender and personal history, there is a cultural context to becoming a parent. Culturally, many things have changed since men waited anxiously listening to women scream during childbirth. In New York City where I work, fathers frequently attend visits to the obstetrician and view sonograms. They talk to their babies and feel them move before they are born. They attend deliveries and sometimes cut the umbilical cord. To the delight of some and the horror of others, sometimes it's "We're pregnant." During this century, there have been significant cultural changes surrounding pregnancy, childbirth, and childcare. Yet, gender differences between men and women, mothers and fathers persist. Sometimes these differences create conflict.

For many parents, becoming a mother or becoming a father became a goal when they were little girls and boys, and continued throughout childhood, teenage years, and young adulthood. They have planned in what ways they will be the same as their own parents and in what ways they will be different. For some parents, the loving parent-child relationships they envision with their own children are replacements for the painful relationships they had or continue to have with theirs. (This was seen in the vignette about Naomi and Wally on page 56.) Other parents rarely or never thought about having children, and have fewer plans or expectations.

For mothers, the care of their babies, the parts delegated and those parts assumed, is primary. All mothers are full-time mothers, including those who have other full-time jobs. The care that babies and young children require is demanding, both emotionally and logistically; the gratifications are immeasurable. Work and child-care conflicts emerge. While her baby or toddler may always be near, feelings of loneliness may increase. Or, in dramatic contrast, as one mother once eloquently and succinctly described, "After my son was born, I never had my mind to myself; he was always in it." I was unsure whether she felt her son was a pleasurable constant companion or a pervasive intruder.

When a woman becomes a mother, the primacy and exclusivity of her romantic relationship with her husband or partner may be influenced by the growing love relationship with her baby. Her partner has competition, if only for her time. A new mother's sexual desire and arousal may vary from being enhanced to being diminished because it is impacted by the physical pleasures and demands of her baby and toddler, as well as by hormonal changes. For men, a woman's pregnancy, labor, delivery, and breastfeeding also have an impact. These experiences can enhance admiration, desire, and intimacy, or diminish it. Becoming parents brings dramatic changes.

Fatherhood has been studied and written about less than motherhood, and over the years many more women than men have been in my groups and consulted with me. However, when observing fathers with their babies, it is obvious that being a father is powerfully gratifying, sometimes surprising, and also stressful. Though mothers are typically the primary caregivers of babies and toddlers, fathers now more than ever also care for their babies and young children. Intimate body care, the ability to soothe a baby, and early father-baby play intensify the early attachment for both. In some families, fathers are the primary caregivers.

Childhood memories shape the image of the kind of parent both mothers and fathers want to be. They influence the childrearing approaches of parents, parent-child interactions, and family life. Parenthood is filled with pleasurable moments of magic derived from the power of love and attachment, and the wonder and satisfaction of watching a baby develop. There are also significant stresses. The intensity and momentum of parent-baby falling-in-love is a motivational force for raising children.

Biomedically, parenthood is possible in increasingly varied ways. IVF, donor sperm, donor egg, and gestational carriers are occurring more frequently. Adoption is also an option. Sometimes ghosts are activated by conception and birth details. Following is Jim, Barbara, and Denise's story.

Jim, Barbara, and Denise "Donor egg, a surrogate, and me, who is the mother . . ."

Jim, referred by a colleague of mine, called to schedule a consultation because he was concerned that his wife Barbara was not bonding with Denise, their 2-month-old daughter. Jim, an architect who worked from home, explained, "I do all of the childcare. Other than giving Denise two bottles a day, Barbara does her editing work. She never holds Denise, changes a diaper, bathes, or plays with her. When we go for a walk, I carry Denise in the snuggly." As we continued to talk, Jim elaborated.

Denise had been conceived with Jim's sperm and an anonymous donor egg. A gestational surrogate carried her to term. Jim and Barbara had tried to conceive for many years and it was determined that Barbara was unable. Jim assured me that Denise was thriving. She slept well and took the bottle well. She had special smiles for daddy. It seemed as though Jim liked being his daughter's primary caretaker, but he knew his wife needed help and that Denise needed her mother. We scheduled an appointment for the following week.

I led Jim, Barbara, and Denise into the parent consultation room: a small, cozy space. A white bulletin board with photographs of babies hangs on one wall above a banquette. A large, open window spanning the adjacent wall looks into the mother-baby playroom. During our initial meeting Denise slept in Jim's arms. Barbara, Jim, and I talked about Denise's conception, gestation, and birth, and how they might be linked to Jim and Barbara's current interactions with her. As we talked, it became increasingly clear to all of us that in some ways Jim and Barbara felt that Denise was Jim's baby, not their baby. For Barbara, being unable to conceive biologically meant that she was not a mother. For Jim, because Denise was conceived with a stranger's egg, and carried and given birth to by another stranger, it was difficult for him to recognize Barbara as Denise's mother. He felt like a single father, which for Jim also meant being Denise's mother. However, for both Jim and Barbara there were events that had occurred many years before and aspects of relationships continuing into the present that had become attached to the details of Denise's conception and birth.

As we talked, Jim held Denise in a snuggly while she slept. Occasionally, he delicately caressed her shoulder. Barbara remained impassive, more in the background. When Denise awakened for her bottle, perhaps related to what we had been talking about, Jim removed her from the snuggly, gently kissed her forehead, and handed her to Barbara. This tender moment indicated the beginning of a readiness for a meaningful shift for the three of them. Jim said, "We want to co-parent."

Denise settled comfortably in Barbara's arms and vigorously sucked the bottle. This picture of an infant feeding in her mother's arms looked typical. However, after Denise finished the bottle, Barbara held her erect at a distance until she burped. She then placed Denise, precariously balanced, across the edge of her lap. Denise looked as if she could slide off her mother's lap at any moment. Barbara seemed to be saying in actions, "She is not my baby, she reminds me of my infertility. I will not hold on to her, I will let Jim take her." Barbara's next comment revealed an additional element of the meaning of her actions on which I would focus: "I want her to be independent." Jim lifted Denise from Barbara's lap and tucked her back into the snuggly. We agreed that I would meet with Barbara and Denise weekly.

The following week, Barbara entered the parents' consultation room with Denise sleeping in the stroller. She sat in the chair closest to the mother-baby playroom. Perhaps this was a precursor to her emerging wish to play with Denise. Barbara continued from where she had left off the previous week. "I have ideas about taking care of a baby that are different than Jim and my mother. Their ways are intrusive and controlling. I think this will interfere with Denise being strong and independent. They want her to be swaddled, I don't. I want her to be free. They give the pacifier to her all the time. I don't want her to have it. I want her to learn to self-soothe. They hold her head all the time; she's strong, she can hold it herself now. They only use the snuggly. I use the stroller. I have nightmares every night."

Barbara had clear ideas about raising Denise that until this moment she had been unable to articulate or effectuate. It now occurred to me that because Barbara was unable to assert these approaches in a constructive way with Denise, her husband, or her mother, who was visiting to help, she either avoided Denise or interacted with her in ways that were misattuned, negligent, or un-empathic. In addition, Barbara was having frequent nightmares. I responded, "It sounds like Jim and your mother are intrusive and controlling not only with Denise, but also with you." Barbara gently and helplessly agreed, "They are, but there's nothing I can do about it. That's the way it's always been." She then added, "Jim was married before and had a baby that died. He divorced shortly after. It was about 20 years ago, but he never really recovered. Denise is important to him. He's very possessive. His baby died in a car accident while his wife was driving." According to Barbara, the death of Jim's baby intensified his lifelong protective, controlling, and caretaking patterns. I wondered whether the death of Jim's baby also intensified Barbara's anxiety about caring for Denise and promoted her wish to please Jim, even if it prevented her from having something she wanted.

It seemed to me that in addition to Barbara's wishes to please her husband and her anxiety about Denise's safety, she also felt unentitled and unable to have any influence on Denise's care. She felt unable to assert her ideas with her mother because she believed it would anger her mother, whose help she needed in order to return to work. Barbara wanted to please both her mother and husband, but also feared Denise would be raised to be "passive and submissive." I now understood her conflict and that it was related to her own passivity.

Some of Barbara's interactions with Denise that looked like neglect and failures of attunement, empathy, and bonding were her attempts to foster strength and independence in Denise, to assert her own independence from both her mother and her husband, and to replace Jim's baby who had died with Denise. I believed that Barbara had felt unentitled and helpless before her infertility, donor egg, and gestational carrier experiences. Her concern for Jim and dependency on her mother were now preventing her from satisfying her own maternal needs. With this complicated history, entwined with the current situation, the most immediate and powerful mechanism to focus on in order to address the problems was her developing relationship with Denise and the pleasures it could bring.

When Denise awakened and cried, Barbara lifted her out of the stroller. Denise immediately stopped crying. I commented, "Denise knows you, she stopped crying as soon as you touched her. She's very well regulated." Over the next several weeks we continued to talk about Barbara's past and current conflicted relationship with her mother, including related childhood memories. We talked about disagreements she had with her husband about Denise's care and her concerns about intensifying her husband's fears of losing Denise. Perhaps most important, we talked about Barbara and Denise. I highlighted aspects of their emerging attuned love relationship, Denise's thriving development, and the merits of Barbara's goals of independence and strength. We talked about age appropriate ways to promote Denise's autonomy. During the next several weeks, Barbara began to take care of Denise and derive pleasure from their interactions.

A turning point had occurred when during our fifth visit, Barbara told me, "The other day after her bottle, Denise was sleeping on my bed and I just watched her. It was wonderful, she looked happy and beautiful." Barbara's description indicated her deepening attachment to Denise and her increased pleasure. Mother-baby falling-in-love was happening.

When Denise was almost 4 months old, I asked Barbara about how she and Denise played together. She matter-of-factly replied, "We don't yet. I'm waiting for her to play." It was as though for Barbara, initiating play with Denise felt intrusive and controlling. The following week when I entered the mother-baby room, Barbara was holding Denise on her lap and face-to-face talking to her. Rather than continuing to wait for Denise to start playing for the first time, Barbara had initiated a singing game, rhythmically kissing her forehead.

Many things had changed for Barbara, Jim, and Denise. Barbara had assumed more care of Denise. Denise was no longer swaddled and did not use the pacifier. At times she was carried in the snuggly and at times pushed in the stroller. Jim and Barbara were both caring for her. Barbara's concerns that Denise would be a passive, weak girl began to fade. She was no longer sliding off Barbara's lap. Barbara's nightmares had stopped. Barbara and Denise joined our mother-baby group. Barbara's concerns about being controlling and intrusive with Denise continued to emerge and to inhibit needed mother-baby interactions.

In some ways, Barbara's long-standing dependency on and submission to her husband and conflicts with her own mother had intensified when combined with the details of Denise's conception and birth. Barbara's deferential and passive style with her husband, and her feelings of inadequacy and anger, had increased, surfaced, and spun out of control in a way that interfered with her early attachment to Denise. Her current dependency on her mother for childcare help had intensified their conflicts. Denise was a trigger that intensified these long-held feelings and relationship difficulties. Our work together enabled Barbara to claim Denise as her baby and assert her goals of independence and strength for Denise in ways that were acceptable to her husband and promoted Denise's development. Barbara's difficulties continued to re-emerge in different ways throughout Denise's early development.

Being a parent occurs in a cultural context in addition to a personal and family context. Many aspects of caring for babies and young children are idealized and others are socially and politically devalued. Throughout history, art, and various aspects of culture, the mother and the father representations have received different amounts and kinds of attention. Fairy-god mother and super-hero father are the most familiar idealized mother and father images. A witch epitomizes the bad mother, and a devil the bad father. It is interesting that these icons are traditionally childless. These artistic and cultural images of good and bad emerge and are sustained because they resonate, though disguised, with childhood memories of actual mothers and fathers. Most adults have access to gratifying and frustrating, protective and frightening, idealized and devalued memories of their own mothers and fathers. Ghosts, and the pleasurable and painful memories they inhabit, create a complex inner world.

Integrating "good" and "bad" mother and father images is sometimes a challenge. Young children face the same challenge. The loving parent-child relationship helps both children and parents integrate the gratifying and pleasurable with the frustrating and hurtful aspects of an individual into one person who has strengths and weaknesses, assets and liabilities. This process is facilitated by the rupture and repair cycles of pleasurable, loving parent-child interactions.

The wish to be a "good mother" is shared by women in a multitude of settings, with endless varieties of backgrounds. It is difficult to define a "good mother." A "good mother" in one culture may not be in another. A protective mother in one family may be considered overprotective in others. Strict can be viewed as mean, and permissive as over-indulgent. A "good mother" for one child may not be good for others. Furthermore, definitions of a "good mother" change over time. In the story that follows, Kathleen had felt like the "worst mother" and her feelings were interfering with her efforts to teach Amber to use the potty.

Kathleen and Amber
"She screams when I take her to the potty . . ."

Sometimes memories haunt parents because of painful associated guilt. The lingering residue of feeling like a bad mother can spread and invade parent-child interactions. Kathleen was unaware this was happening to her when she was trying to teach Amber to use the potty.

Kathleen and Amber were in the pre-nursery mother-child program. It was early spring and yellow tulips could be seen through the playroom window. Amber was now 3 years old. She had freckles and long red hair tied into a ponytail. She was physically agile and strong. Kathleen had described in detail how Amber rode her bright-red scooter through the park, weaving skillfully around obstacles and pedestrians. Amber was as competent verbally as she was athletic. She was generally easy-going and adaptive. Developmental steps from bottle to cup and crib to bed had gone smoothly. However, none of these abilities or traits was helping Amber learn to use the potty.

Kathleen described her hopelessness to the mothers' group. "I will never teach her. She just won't do it. She seems terrified. She screams every time I take her to the potty." Listening to Kathleen, I was reminded that when Amber was 16 months old she had symptoms of a urinary tract infection. After a week of home remedies of cranberry juice and crying when she urinated, the pediatrician convinced Kathleen that catheterizing Amber was necessary in order to make a diagnosis. Kathleen had not thought that Amber had an infection and was concerned about the impact of this painful and invasive medical procedure, but with her husband's urging, she consented.

The procedure was even worse than Kathleen had anticipated. She and two nurses held Amber down while she screamed in pain and terror. Kathleen wept. The lab results confirmed that Amber did not have a urinary tract infection. Kathleen felt excruciatingly guilty for having agreed to the procedure even though the doctor had said it was essential and her husband had insisted.

Several weeks after the procedure, feeling very guilty and like "the worst mother in the world," Kathleen had confided in the mothers' group that she had not told the doctor or her husband about Amber's "genital rubbing." She had believed it had caused some irritation and had triggered the urinary tract infection symptoms. In retrospect she had wondered whether her embarrassment about Amber's masturbation and genital pleasure had prevented her from telling the doctor. She thought that if the doctor had known, he might not have suggested the catheterization. Kathleen believed she was a "bad mother," not only because she had not told the doctor, but also because her daughter was masturbating.

As Kathleen described the current struggle wrestling Amber to the potty screaming, I reminded her about the medical procedure when Amber was 16 months old. "It sounds like when you take Amber to the potty, in your mind you are taking her to be catheterized again. It is as though you are not remembering, but you are re-living all the terror, horror, and guilt you experienced.

In addition, there may be more for us to talk about children's sex-play." Even though it is not clear how or whether all that was in Kathleen's mind was communicated to Amber, and it is not known what Amber's own associations were between the potty and her medical procedure when she was younger, there seemed to be some connections.

The relief Kathleen and the entire group experienced upon hearing my comment about sex-play was palpable. Understanding what was happening in the present in terms of memories of the past was liberating. Kathleen now understood that for her, taking Amber to the potty felt like a re-living of the past medical procedure and all the associated feelings. I also thought that her guilt about the catheterization was compounded by her own residual sexual guilt that had been reactivated. I asked, "What childhood memories do you have about masturbation?" Kathleen remembered that when she was around 10 years old her parents forbid her to touch her genitals. However, she secretly did masturbate to orgasm in her bed before falling asleep and felt deeply ashamed. As an adult, Kathleen knew that childhood genital exploration and rubbing and adult masturbation are considered normal; yet, her own childhood sexual guilt had been reactivated. The way in which Kathleen's new understanding of her memories influenced her interactions with Amber is unclear; however, Amber no longer cried about the potty.

Kathleen's unrecognized lingering sexual guilt and shame, which was imbedded in her story, could now be discussed in the group. Each woman recounted experiences of her own childhood sex-play, teenage sexuality, and her parents' reactions. We also talked about attitudes the women and their husbands had toward their children's current genital curiosity and pleasure. Amber began to routinely use the potty. Kathleen became more self-forgiving.

Childhood sexual guilt that persists into adulthood is common. One of the women in the group told us about an experience she had as a college student. She regularly studied in the school library sitting in front of a locked bookcase with glass doors. The books kept behind the locked doors were about sex. One day the doors were unlocked. With some anxiety and much excitement, when the librarian was not looking, she took out a book. She was amazed by the pictures and incredibly relieved to discover that masturbation was normal for boys and girls, men and women.

The idealized mother is a wish fulfilling fantasy. For some women, the mother they want to be is unattainable because it is an idealized, wished for mother left over from childhood. The idealized mother is like the fairytale mother who is always gratifying. She never gets angry, tired, overwhelmed, bored, or busy with things other than her child. She never makes mistakes. She protects her child from all physical and emotional pain. If she recognizes the impossibility of achieving these idealized goals, she idealizes her ability to adapt when she fails. An idealized mother fantasy can never be an actual mother.

Some women believe they will never themselves be as good mothers as their own mothers. Their own mothers are idealized. This can occur for different reasons and play out in different ways. Viewing their own mothers as ideal protects them from acknowledging the flaws in their own mothers, and the accompanying hurt and anger they experienced as children and may continue to feel. The idealization may seem to be or may actually be needed to preserve a valued adult mother-daughter relationship. Some grandmothers implicitly demand the status of "best mother." The grandchildren fill an emptiness created by retirement or loneliness, and being the idealized mother is a comfort.

The "bad mother" is an idea in stark contrast to the "ideal mother." The wicked stepmother of childhood fairytales embodies the "bad mother" and lurks. Sometimes, childhood memories of an actual mother exude danger or even evil, the essence of a witch. Fear or hate may accompany these memories. A mother's dread, conscious and unconscious, about being or appearing to be a witch mother can hover and at times intrude into conscious awareness and action. Fear of being a witch mother can sometimes inhibit needed limit-setting. In some ways, perhaps for all mothers, the personal good-mother-self/bad-mother-self pendulum swings and exerts influence on the parent-child relationship.

Integrating the "good mother" she wishes to be with the actual mother she is is an ongoing process. This process includes the rupture and repair cycles in mother-child loving interactions and the range and fluctuations of associated feelings. This process means recognizing and accepting that she will be a mother whom she views as her best at times and her worst at other times. The notion of the "good enough mother" becomes a useful concept. The "good enough mother" (a term coined by Donald Winnicott) provides sufficient amounts of gratification and frustration, attunement, and failures of attunement. And while an equation for "sufficient amounts" does not exist, an important element is that rupture and repair cycles of mother-child loving interactions become stabilized and expected, and loving pleasurable feelings predominate.

Parents, like children, often feel that they are bad when they are angry. Parents get angry with their children and then return to loving feelings and interactions. Parents get distracted from their children and then turn their full attention to them. Parents make mistakes and correct them. Confidence in the cyclical nature of relationships mitigates feeling like a bad parent.

Almost every mother has had the experience of taking a leisurely walk on a beautiful day, having a lovely meal in a child-friendly restaurant, grocery shopping to provide delicious food to her family, or flying to a long-awaited holiday destination with a toddler who suddenly bursts into an all-out screaming and kicking temper tantrum. Mothers' temperatures rise and heart rates accelerate. It feels like all eyes are on her and she is being designated the worst mother.

Feeling like a bad mother is sometimes linked to career ambitions, work schedules, and the pursuit of interests and relationships other than children. In the following story, being a mother and also having a successful career was a challenge for Ricky.

Ricky and Brianna
"I love my career, I'm a terrible mother . . ."

Ricky had waited to become pregnant until she felt that she could not wait any longer. She had worked hard since getting her MBA and had built a successful retail business. She loved her work and was eager to keep growing her business. Ricky was now 43 years old and Brianna was 20 months. Ricky thought the mother-child program was perfect, but she was not sure how often she would attend the mothers' group because of work. Work may have been one of her reasons; being a single mother, though not mentioned, may have been another. Ricky avoided talking about it. We arranged for Brianna's babysitter to accompany her when Ricky was unavailable.

Ricky did everything fast. She talked, moved, and thought fast. Everything she said and did had a lively, exuberant style. Her eyes twinkled and her golden hair bounced, reflecting the light as she moved. She repeatedly gave directions to Brianna: "Say hello." "Give your friend a kiss." "Go play." She also posed many rhetorical questions to me, "Isn't she adorable?" "Don't you think she's the cutest?" "Isn't she so smart?" Brianna, trying to keep up, looked dazed.

Ricky and Brianna had been in the program since September. It was now early December. Ricky had brought Brianna to every playgroup, stayed about 10 minutes, and then left. Brianna's slight smile rapidly faded when her mother slipped out the door.

Throughout the playgroup, Brianna softly sobbed and wandered aimlessly around the playroom, often gazing out the window into the courtyard where she had seen her mother walk away. She was unable to play or to be comforted by the playgroup leaders. Since mothers' groups at the Center are for mothers only, Brianna's babysitter remained in the playroom observation area in order to be available to Brianna, but mostly she spent the hour on her phone. Brianna and the babysitter seemed emotionally disconnected. I later learned that Ricky felt competitive with the babysitter and preferred that she and Brianna not have a "close relationship." Brianna's language was now delayed for her age. Ricky had repeatedly refused any additional help for Brianna or for herself.

We had just returned from winter vacation and for the first time Ricky attended the entire mothers-group. She had become concerned about Brianna after observing a friend's child who was the same age. "My friend's little girl can do so many things Brianna can't do. I'm worried." Brianna was now 23 months old. Ricky agreed to supplement the playgroup with weekly individual play sessions for Brianna with her playgroup leader, Alyson, and at the same time, in the same playroom, Ricky and I would talk. With her mother present and available while she played with Alyson, Brianna would be more comfortable and would be able to build a relationship with Alyson that would be helpful when she was in the playgroup without her mother and needed someone with whom to feel emotionally connected. In addition, my talking with Ricky might help us to understand more about Brianna, Ricky, and the babysitter.

During our first three meetings, Ricky and I talked while we watched Brianna begin to play with Alyson. Alyson's exclusive attention to Brianna, the lowered stimulation without the other children in the playroom, and most important, Ricky remaining close and available, enabled Brianna to feel more comfortable, trust Alyson, and for them to begin to play together. While Ricky remained available to Brianna, she described to me the details of her enjoyable interactions with Brianna. She highlighted bath-time games, reading, and breakfast time. Ricky also talked about her pride in Brianna's physical appearance. Brianna had long, blond hair, a rosy complexion, ice blue eyes, and delicate features. While talking about these positive, gratifying aspects of Brianna and pleasure in their relationship, Ricky was implicitly asserting some positive features about herself as a mother. Ricky conveyed her anxiety about Brianna's development and her mothering by her repeated rhetorical question, "She's so smart, isn't she?" Since Ricky's work was important to her and often kept her away from Brianna, the absence of any mention of work was potentially meaningful. In addition, her avoidance of mentioning anything about being a single mother was noteworthy.

At the end of our fourth session there was a shift. Ricky began to comment on the pleasure and significance of our conversations together. "It's amazing how we talk about all the little things she does." Focusing with me on the "little things" she knew about Brianna and enjoyed with her enabled Ricky to begin to talk about her conflict and guilt about time away from Brianna, the anxiety she felt when separated from her, and the conviction that she was a "terrible mother."

Upon arriving at the Center the following week, Brianna refused to enter the playroom. She was kicking and screaming. Ricky was reprimanding her and threatening to leave without her. Clearly disturbed by Brianna's behavior, Ricky began to tell me about the fun they had together on the bus ride to the Center and her belief that Brianna did not want their play together to end. I thought this was also true about Ricky, who preferred to continue to play with Brianna rather than to resume our conversation about her feeling like a "bad mother."

I asked Ricky what it was like playing with Brianna on the way to the Center. She responded, "We have a lot of fun. I exaggerate everything. I speak loud and fast, it's exhausting, but it helps me to stay focused on her and not be preoccupied with my work." In the same way as Ricky tried to keep work out of her mind when with Brianna, she also kept work and being a single mother out of our conversation. Ricky's ability to reflect on aspects of herself when she interacted with Brianna was impressive. It gave me the opportunity to address something I thought might be important. I commented, "The kind of play you are describing, although a strain, also sounds like it is serving an important function. It seems vital to you to keep a constant focus on Brianna while you are with her. What would it be like to be with Brianna if you were not talking to her for a moment, if you were thinking about something you needed to do at work and Brianna was quietly looking out the window?" In a surprised and quiet voice, Ricky reflected, "You mean that could be ok?" I understood Ricky's question to echo her surprise that she can be a good mother even while thinking about work. I thought to myself that this might enable Ricky to be more attuned and emotionally available to Brianna, rather than blindly or in a way compulsively focused on her.

The next session, Ricky and Brianna entered the playroom ready to play. The change in Ricky was telling. Ricky seemed more relaxed and her voice was gentle. She made no demands on Brianna or on me. She described her trip to the Center as "pleasant." "Sometimes I talked to Brianna and sometimes I was thinking about work."

Ricky became more aware of and attuned to Brianna's inner world and to her own. Her focus shifted from external behavioral attending to Brianna, to emotional connecting with Brianna. These changes in Ricky remained and expanded. These changes also enabled Ricky to help the babysitter to be more emotionally available to Brianna during the playgroup, as well as at other times. Ricky's feelings about being a bad mother no longer influenced her rivalry with the babysitter in a way that had prevented her from helping the babysitter to be more attentive to Brianna. Ricky insisted that the babysitter not use her cell phone while taking care of Brianna and limit screen-time for Brianna. In addition, Ricky's increased attunement to Brianna provided a useful model for the babysitter.

During our next six sessions, Brianna's play became more focused and organized. During her playgroup, she no longer cried; her relationship with Alyson was secure, which helped her when her mother left. Brianna turned to Alyson when she needed help and to share the pleasure of her play. She always chose to sit next to Alyson during snack. Brianna also was able to remain emotionally connected to her babysitter, who had put her cell phone away during the playgroup. With a glance across the room or up-close touching base, they stayed connected. With her mother and babysitter's support, and her relationship with Alyson, Brianna was able to participate in the playgroup. Her pleasure in her social interactions with the other children and delight in play activities was apparent. Expressive language began to emerge. The individual sessions with me and Alyson were no longer needed.

Ricky had been reluctant to participate in the mothers' group in part because of her general devaluation of women – she had more important things to do, as well as her competition with them that was related to her painful feelings about being a "bad mother." Pleased with Brianna's development and feeling more supported in both her work and her mothering, Ricky became less self-critical. She began to attend the mothers group occasionally. In time, Ricky began to talk about her childhood memories and her experience of being a single mother. Feeling like a "good enough mother" had needed to occur first.

Our individual sessions had enabled Ricky to share with me the details of the pleasurable moments she had with Brianna and her sense of pride in Brianna's physical appearance – both of which reflected some positive although fragile feelings about herself as a "good enough mother." These enhanced feelings about herself as a mother enabled Ricky to reflect on aspects of her interactions with Brianna that were overstimulating, emotionally disconnected, and unsatisfying to them both. My recognizing the importance of her work and acknowledging her professional achievements supported another important part of her life which she had felt she needed to keep out of her mind while she was with Brianna. My raising the question about what it would be like to be with Brianna while thinking about work prompted her to question what had been an unconscious tenet: I must be completely focused on Brianna when I am with her. Ricky was now able to relinquish that notion and to better integrate these two parts of her life, being a mother and her career. This integration, combined with a more positive view of herself as a mother, decreased her need to ward off thoughts about work while with Brianna and enabled her to be more attuned, rather than rigidly focused. Brianna began to thrive.

Single parenthood, by choice or otherwise, is arrived at for a multitude of reasons, has individual impact on parents, and for Ricky, remained in the background of our work together.

A woman's relationship with her own mother, in actuality and in her mind, may change when she becomes a mother. Her primary mother-child relationship identity shifts from "I am the daughter of my mother" to "I am the mother of my child." A leap in independence may occur with this shift, while at the same time dependency needs may increase. A mother's ability to see the world from her own mother's point of view may also increase. Mothers and daughters now share a momentous life experience. In the following story, Sally had an insight. She realized that her mother might have felt differently about her needs for comfort than Sally had believed for her entire life.

Sally and Cliff
"He won't sleep in his own bed . . ."

Sally and Cliff were in the pre-nursery mother-child program. Cliff was a thriving 30-month-old little boy. He ate well, spoke well, played well, and slept well. For the past 3 weeks he had awakened happy every morning in his mother and father's bed. Every morning, his mother Sally was surprised. She never heard or felt him get into their bed during the night.

Sally did not think that this was a good pattern for Cliff. Sally's husband did not share her view, but deferred to her. Sally was convinced there was nothing she could do about it; she never felt or heard Cliff enter their bed. She only discovered him in the morning. "What can I do about it? I sleep through it." The discrepancy between Sally's conviction that it was not good for Cliff to come into their bed and her equally strong conviction that there was nothing she could do about it suggested to me that there might be childhood memories connected to what I understood to be her unconscious conflict about changing it. Ghosts had been activated.

In order to understand more, I asked Sally about the value there was for her and her husband having Cliff sleep in bed with them; she said, "I'm providing him with needed security and we all get a good night's sleep." While Sally acknowledged value in Cliff sleeping in their bed, she still insisted that she wanted him in his own bed. "But what can I do, I sleep through it?"

When someone insists that they want to do something, but they themselves create the obstacle to doing it, something may be obscured. Sally's repeated phrase, "What can I do, I sleep through it?" offered a possible clue. I asked, "Who slept through what when you were a child?" Sally responded, "When I was a little girl, I had nightmares about our house burning down. I was terrified. Every night I would sneak to my parents' bedroom and sleep on the floor outside their closed door. I didn't want to wake them. My parents suffered enough. They slept through it every night."

I had already learned from prior discussions in the mothers' group that protecting Sally's parents from her fears was a major theme in her relationship with her parents, especially with her mother. Sally had always been determined to be a "good girl." Her mother had severe migraines and her parents seemed to live in constant fear that a migraine would be triggered. Precautions were always being taken. Sally's mother often retired to her bedroom and demanded not to be disturbed. When Sally was a little girl and awoke in the middle of the night, she dared not enter her parents' bedroom.

I responded to Sally's dilemma, "The current situation sounds like a repetition of your experience as a child sleeping outside your parents' bedroom." Sally looked surprised and bewildered. I continued, "The roles are now reversed and Cliff is getting something you didn't get. You are now the parent sleeping through your child's distress rather than the scared child sleeping alone on the floor. And Cliff is the scared child getting a comfort that you did not get when you were a little girl." I then added, "In spite of this, like you, Cliff's distress is not being addressed directly." Sally looked stunned with the connection between her past and the present.

The following week Sally told us in the mothers' group that she had begun to hear Cliff when he got into her bed in the middle of the night. In many ways this seemed magical, because how it occurred could not be explained. Cliff was being awakened by frightening dreams. Sally was now able to walk him back to his own bed and comfort him. During the day, they talked about the frightening dreams. Within two weeks, Cliff was sleeping through the night in his own bed again.

Sally's insight that a childhood memory was being enacted, though not clear how, enabled her to hear Cliff in the middle of the night. Now a mother, her revived memory of sleeping outside her parent's bedroom helped her to separate her own childhood wish to get into her parents' bed, or second-best, to sleep on the floor outside their bedroom, from her current interactions with Cliff. She recognized that what Cliff needed was understanding and comfort that could be achieved out of her bed. In addition, Sally now believed that her childhood memory was about what she thought her mother wanted. She entertained the possibility that her mother would have wanted to know about her distress and to soothe her. "I didn't want to disturb my mother. I'm not sure what she would have wanted." Sally's childhood memory had slightly, but meaningfully, changed.

The next story is a dramatic example of the resiliency of mother-baby attachment and love during a stressful time and maternal depression.

Doris and Mackenzie
"She discovered her bellybutton . . ."

February snow was blanketing the city as it blustered through the cold, windy streets. The warm, bubbling excitement of the mothers who had weathered the storm filled the mother-baby room. The despair on Doris's face matched the bleak winter chill that seeped through the window-frame gaps. Doris was new to the mothers' group that had been meeting since October. Three months earlier, Doris had learned that her husband had been having an affair for almost 2 years. He now wanted a divorce. For the last several months, a psychiatrist had been treating Doris with medication for depression.

Doris entered the mother-baby room, placed 9-month-old Mackenzie in front of a toy shelf, and walked away. She sat outside the warmth of the mothers' close gathering. As Doris sat alone, she ignored Mackenzie's attempts to approach her and rejected any suggestions from me that Mackenzie wanted to be close to her. Doris disagreed with my idea that Mackenzie might be reacting to a new setting with strangers and wanting to be close to her mother for security and comfort. Doris continued to shun Mackenzie's efforts to be held or even to touch. Doris looked distraught. Mackenzie looked sad.

Two months earlier, Doris had stopped making entries in Mackenzie's photo album. She had delegated most of Mackenzie's care to a babysitter and no longer played with her. It seemed to me, with all the painful and humiliating rejection and rage Doris had been experiencing with her husband, it was impossible for her to realize that Mackenzie wanted to be close to her, emotionally or physically. A rupture in their emotional attachment had occurred.

For the next 3 weeks during the mothers' group, at every possible opportunity, I drew attention to the behavior of the babies that indicated their growing love and emotional attachment to their mothers. Glances from across the room, climbing into mothers' laps for cuddles, seeking comfort when needed and being soothed, bringing toys to their mothers, shared smiles and mutual gaze: behaviors that accompany feelings of emotional connectedness and psychological attachment. There were many opportunities to identify and describe these mother-baby interactions during the group. Whenever Mackenzie looked at her mother, even if only a fleeting glance, or made any attempt to get close to her, I highlighted it. "I think when Mackenzie looks at you while she is playing, she wants to know if you saw what she did." Or, "I think Mackenzie got startled and wants to be close to you."

Doris continued to criticize and ridicule Mackenzie's typical attachment behaviors. "It's weird when she hangs on me, or tries to climb on me. It's strange when Mackenzie clings to me. I hate it when she touches my hair, what's wrong with her?" While Doris was insistent, I persisted, "You've been so hurt and rejected by your husband, it's hard for you to feel that Mackenzie wants to be close to you, or that Mackenzie loves you." At other times I noted, "Maybe Mackenzie reminds you of your husband, how angry you are at him, and how much you want to hurt him."

Four weeks after joining the group, Doris entered the mother-baby room with a slight smile and for the first time sat close to Mackenzie, who reached out and touched her several times. In striking contrast to the past, Doris did not recoil. I wondered about the meaning of this change. When Mackenzie settled on her mother's lap for the first time, Doris tentatively asked me a question that revealed an emerging fantasy that corresponded to the changes in their interactions. Doris hesitantly said, "Mackenzie has discovered her belly button. She plays with it all the time. Do you think she remembers when she was attached to me by the umbilical cord before she was born?" I responded, "It sounds like you feel that Mackenzie loves you and wants to be close to you."

I did not validate the idea proposed by Doris that Mackenzie remembered being attached to the umbilical cord, nor did I deny it. I addressed what I thought to be the meaning of her question. I affirmed, "Mackenzie loves you and wants to be physically close and wants to feel emotionally connected."

Maternal depression and painful current life events can disrupt early mother-baby attachment. It was difficult for Doris to repair the mutually nurturing mother-baby relationship with Mackenzie that had been ruptured a few months earlier. My conviction about Mackenzie's attachment and love helped lessen Doris's feelings of being unlovable that had been triggered by her husband's rejection. She was now able to enjoy the rewards of mother-baby love even in the context of the painful, humiliating rejection she was experiencing. Doris resumed entries in Mackenzie's photo album.

Some combination of the gratifying mother-baby interactions Doris was now having with Mackenzie, the anti-depression medication she had been prescribed by her psychiatrist, and the synergies between them had helped to both alleviate her depression and to promote attuned mother-baby interactions that supported Mackenzie's development and Doris's recovery.

Marlene and George "He thinks the nanny is his mother . . ."

Being a parent creates powerful motivation and new abilities to resolve internal and interpersonal difficulties. Recovery from trauma is now possible in a new way, in a new love relationship. Revived horrors and fears related to childhood memories of illness and death may clash with becoming a mother. In the following story, Marlene is caught in a reliving of the past and an unconscious associated dread. In many ways she was relinquishing her baby, George.

Marlene was an exceptionally beautiful and professionally successful woman. She was tall and slim, with long, blond hair cascading down her back. She always looked elegant, whether wearing jeans or a simple black dress. Marlene was a fashion model. George, 10 months old, was physically robust and sturdy. His blond hair framed his angelic face. At a glance everything looked perfect. However, this superficially perfect picture was blemished. Each week Marlene carried George into the mother-baby room, placed him on the floor next to a toy shelf, and walked to the other side of the room to sit. They remained at a distance throughout the group. They never touched and George never looked at his mother. From a distance, Marlene frequently gazed longingly at George. I wondered about the meaning of what I was observing.

George was a competent crawler and was able to pull himself to standing. He was physically capable, though he rarely moved from where his mother had placed him. It seemed as though if he moved from where he had last been with her, he would completely lose the ability to find his mother again. In the playroom, George drooled excessively; his chin and cheeks were always smeared with saliva that dribbled down and soaked his shirt. George had little interest in exploring toys. He appeared uninterested in the other babies. Both George and Marlene seemed sad.

During the third time the mother-baby group met, Marlene revealed, "I feel like I'm not George's mother. He thinks his nanny is his mother; I've turned his care almost completely over to her. She's with him more than I am. He laughs with her in a way that he never laughs with me." In some ways Marlene took responsibility for George thinking the nanny was his mother. She had turned his care over to the nanny and she acknowledged that she did not feel like George's mother. Marlene implied that she was being reactive to George. She was unaware about what was motivating her to distance herself from George. I believed that for Marlene, joining a mothers' group meant that she could qualify as a mother, even if she did not feel like George's mother. Ghosts were emerging.

Marlene quickly became an active member of the group. She was eager to recount memories of her own childhood. She was the youngest of three children whose mother had died when Marlene was 15 years old after a long, painful, and disfiguring illness. While Marlene spoke about her memories of her mother and events after her death, I began to wonder whether for Marlene, becoming a mother herself meant becoming sick, ugly, and then dying as her mother had. I shared this idea with Marlene. "I wonder if you have mixed feelings about being a mother. You love George and want to be his mother, but being a mother may also frighten you. Being a mother may also mean getting sick and dying like your mother." My words seemed to hover quietly over the mothers and babies, and resonate with the tear that floated down Marlene's cheek.

Over the next several months, as the mothers in the group talked about their own mothers, Marlene told us about the sad, horrifying details of her mother's illness and death, and how much more she missed her since George was born. Perhaps in some ways feeling that she was like her mother had helped her to feel close to her mother, even though it also frightened her and distanced her from George. Happy, pleasurable memories also began to emerge. Glowing smiles lit up and animated her face. Mourning was resumed. It included her sad and frightening memories, happy loving memories, and healthy images of her mother. Marlene's tears dried. Becoming a mother became unlinked from dying.

Gradually, Marlene assumed more of George's care. She frequently bathed him. She ate breakfast with him every morning before going to work, and frequently dinner. Marlene and George began to play together. Marlene also began to tuck him into his crib at bedtime. Perhaps most meaningful, she made up what became their special bedtime song. Psychologically, Marlene became George's mother. George thrived. The drooling that had drenched his face and shirt no longer flowed. Of course, George was older, but perhaps something that had changed between George and his mother also had an impact on his drooling.

Parents delight as they watch their babies grow during their first 3 years. The maturational leaps that typically occur are wondrous. A baby's first smiles, first steps, and first words are enchanting. A baby's boundless energy and a toddler's endless curiosity are captivating.

When postpartum depression occurs as it did with Doris (p. 81), the experience of becoming a mother is altered. The typical stresses are overwhelming. The anxiety is incapacitating. The potential for mothering pleasure and satisfaction is diminished or obliterated. When becoming a father is overwhelming, men may flee in a variety of ways. For these mothers and fathers, professional psychiatric help may be needed.

6 Creating Shared Memory Narratives

Parents and their children co-create shared memory narratives. Together they remember and construct stories about actual events. Memory narratives organize the inner world of thoughts and feelings: the joy, the sorrow, and the fear, the love, the anger, and the pride. Memory narratives consolidate adaptation. Young children with rudimentary language need their parents' help to construct narratives. During the co-construction process, the parents influence the content of the child's memory. The children are not alone with the experience that the memory represents. This is the beginning of a life-long process of narrating and sharing lived experience, and the comfort and pleasure it brings.

The developmental sequence that precedes memory narrative co-construction begins with pointing. Babies point and engage parents in a shared focus of attention to an observable object. This milestone signals an important leap in a baby's development. The baby has discovered that each object is a thing that has a name and can be the focus of shared attention. A baby's pointing is a complex communication. It is evidence of the interpersonal nature of the baby's developing mind.

A baby pointing, often accompanied with the sound "eh" or "dis" in English-speaking families, and the parents' response it elicits, is an interaction that externalizes or makes explicit the internal experience of a shared focus of attention. The parent and the baby delight in recognition of each other's mind. It is an experience of inter-subjectivity like mutual gaze, shared smiles, and social referencing. Both the parent and the child know they are referencing the same thing. This interpersonal, inter-subjective experience is so compelling and pleasurable to a baby that it is repeated many times a day.

Sometimes pointing means, "I want that." For example, 1-year-old Wynn points to a book, meaning, "Daddy, I want that book." Her father responds by handing the book to her. Other times the goal of pointing is exclusively to create a joint focus of attention. Wynn points to a book, her father hands the book to her, she repeats the pointing but this time to another book, her father hands the other book to her, she repeats the pointing to yet another book again, and again, and again. The meaning of this pointing is not to get the book but to create a joint focus of attention interaction between the child and the parent. They look together at an object chosen by the baby, agree on the word that represents the object, and enjoy the inter-subjective experience of knowing they are referencing the same object. A clear example, because the object cannot be held, is the following. Wynn points to the clock on the wall and says "clock," signaling, "Mommy, I see that. It's called a clock. Do you see it too, do you call it a clock?" This pointing gesture invites her mother to look at the clock, and to let Wynn know that she sees it also, and also calls it a clock. Wynn's mother says some version of, "Yes, that's a clock, I see the clock too." The conversation is confirming they are looking at the same thing and use the same word to represent it. They are thinking about the clock together. It is initiated by the baby pointing and confirmed with words, gaze, and an inter-subjective knowing. During this phase of development, these kinds of interactions are repeated frequently with great joy. The next developmental step is when shared attention is to a thing or an event that is not observable but is being remembered and thought about together. Creating shared memory narratives then begins to emerge.

Remembering together is a symbolic pointing to a past event. The event or object cannot be seen currently; it can only be remembered or thought about. Remembering together creates a shared focus of attention to a mental process.

Sharing memories with parents during the narrative co-construction process helps the children's remembering to be adaptive: it helps them to organize their inner world and to structure lived experience into memories. The selection of events that are included in the narrative has an impact on the usefulness of the memory to master trauma, savor pleasure, and to create and sustain a positive sense of self and continuity-of-being in the context of a specific experience. The foundation of an organized inner world with emotional content is being constructed, and an autobiographical narrative process is beginning.

For example, when Dex was 16 months old, he and his father said "bye-bye" to Dex's mother, who was leaving the apartment. In his father's arms, Dex waved to his mother at the door. They all said "bye-bye." When the door closed, Dex began to cry, "Mama." His father reminded him, "Mommy went bye-bye; she will be home soon." Then, they began to play. Ten minutes later Dex said, "Mama." His father remembered with him again what had occurred. "You remember, Mama went bye-bye." Dex repeated, "Bye-bye." Twenty minutes later, the interaction was repeated. Thirty minutes later, mommy came home; they had a happy reunion. After a half hour of play Dex's parents announced, "It's naptime." Dex ran and hid under the table. His mother played, "Where's Dex, I don't see him?" His father joined in, "Where's Dex? Bye-bye, Dex." Dex then popped out from under the table with a big smile. Together with pleasure in pretend play, they were all remembering the earlier separation without the tears and with Dex now doing the leaving rather than being left. His mother then said, "I think you are remembering when I went out this morning. We said bye-bye, you cried, then you played with daddy. After a while I came home. Now it's nap time."

In this example, Dex's contribution to the co-constructed memory was hiding under the table. He was acting out in play the memory of separation from his mother. He did not want the separation repeated with a nap. His parents provided the narrative and included his reaction to the separation. This is an example of the beginning of parents and children creating shared memory narratives.

Parents often wish that their children would not remember certain events because they were so awful or painful, as well as guilt- or shame-inducing to the parents. Parents may be convinced by well-meaning others that children will not remember. In some ways, wishing or believing that children will not remember substitutes for wishing the event had never happened. When an event is not remembered explicitly with a narrative, it is remembered implicitly with a triggered repetition of the feelings. In this way, the event is re-lived instead of being remembered. Remembering how something felt is different than feeling it again. Remembering something that was painful is less stressful than re-living it.

When parents wish something had never happened, they might think that putting the event and the accompanying feelings into words makes it worse, makes it more real. In fact, the opposite is true: putting the event and feelings into words, creating a shared memory narrative, can make the remembered images and feelings more manageable. The child is not alone with the memory. "Mommy and daddy were with me" is a valuable part of a child's memory of a stressful event.

An important part of many events for children is their parents' emotional response to the event. Parents crying in the emergency room and yelling at the doctor can be more disturbing than the injury itself. Including parents' reactions in the shared memory narrative helps children to manage the feelings and to adapt. The words while remembering together, "Mommy was so angry and yelled at the doctor" help the child to remember in a new context an event that when it was occurring had been filled with overwhelming, uncontrollable rage and fear. The new context is the parent's self-reflection. This new context helps the child remember the event and the feelings, rather than re-experience the feelings.

Including feelings from the child's perspective in the memory narrative is important in order to enable children to use the memory to adapt to the event. Sometimes the most stressful part of an event is omitted from the narrative. For example, being restrained to get sutures may be more frightening for a young child, and also for the parents, than the sutures. Seeing masked people in the operating room may be more frightening than the impending surgery. Including the most stressful parts of an experience in the co-constructed memory narrative is valuable.

Tamara was almost 3 years old when she cut off her long, beautiful hair. She cut it short and completely uneven. Her mother, Mary Jane, was furious and let Tamara know it. Mary Jane told me how she yelled at Tamara, "Look what you've done. You are a mess. You've ruined your long, beautiful hair." For Mary Jane it was as if Tamara was no longer the little girl she loved and valued.

It was as if her long, beautiful hair had made her lovable. Mary Jane despaired, "I'm so angry, I can't even look at her." Mary Jane began to recognize that her angry response was intensified out of proportion because she had used Tamara's beautiful ponytail as a symbolic repair of her own hated, short, and graying hair, in addition to assuaging her other feelings of inadequacy. This insight tempered Mary Jane's rage at Tamara.

According to Mary Jane, the only way Tamara looked decent now was when her hair was tied into two short ponytails. However, Tamara was refusing to wear ponytails (which had been her favorite hairstyle). This only changed when Mary Jane remembered that when Tamara had cut her hair, it had been in a ponytail. For Tamara, wearing a ponytail had become a trigger for the memory of cutting her hair which was forbidden, being frightened by her mother's angry reprimand, and perhaps also was a reminder of her mother's overvaluation of her long hair – all of which had become linked to wearing a ponytail. Mary Jane was now able to create a useful memory narrative with Tamara.

Mary Jane began the conversation, "I guess when you cut your hair when it was in a ponytail, you were curious about what it would feel like, how it would look, and how I would react. I was so startled that I yelled so loud and said some not so nice things. I must have really frightened you and made you feel terrible. I'm sorry." The memory narrative Tamara and Mary Jane created together included Tamara's understandable curiosity about cutting her hair that had been in a ponytail when she cut it, her mother's angry reaction, and the fear it evoked. The idea that her hair would grow back was also included in the memory narrative. Tamara resumed wearing ponytails.

When a child adds something to the co-constructed parent-child memory narrative that is inconsistent with the parent's memory of the event, understanding the meaning of the child's addition is important. When Charlie was 3 years old he had his tonsils removed. According to his mother, part of his post-operative care included electrodes being attached to his chest. Charlie wanted them off, but needed to wait until the doctor removed them. After the surgery, when Charlie and his mother were creating a shared memory narrative about his hospitalization, surgical procedure, and numerous blood tests, Charlie insisted that he had pulled the electrodes off himself. Perhaps this was Charlie's way of saying, "I wasn't a totally passive, helpless boy; I did something that I wanted to do."

Joanna, Stanley, and Cody's story that follows is about a frightening accident that triggered profound guilt and anger for the parents, and a traumatic reaction for the child. It illustrates a turbulent journey to the creation of a shared memory narrative that was reparative for the entire family.

Joanna, Stanley, and Cody "There was blood everywhere . . ."

Cody was almost 3 years old. She had gone to sleep at 7:30 pm and awoke an hour later unable to return to sleep. Her mother Joanna was reading in the living room when Cody walked in, cuddling her pink bunny and looking adorable. "Mommy, I can't sleep. Is daddy home yet?" Joanna decided to let Cody play in the living room while they waited for Cody's father Stanley; he had been expected before Cody went to sleep.

Cody was excited, that familiar, over-excited, gleeful state children get into when they are allowed to stay up late to wait for daddy. Jumping on the living room sofa, Cody fell and cut her forehead on the corner of the coffee table. She cried in a way Joanna had never heard before: a loud mixture of fear and pain. There was blood on the floor, sofa, and coffee table. Cody's nightgown was splattered with blood. Joanna could not see where the blood was coming from. She was overwhelmed and terrified. She shrieked helplessly, frozen for several moments until she gained control and called an ambulance. Within 10 minutes, Cody and Joanna, now stunned silent, were in the ambulance racing through the streets. The blaring siren pierced the ambulance's interior quiet.

Cody's father, Stanley, met them at the hospital 15 minutes later. Tears streaked Joanna's face and horror engulfed her as she restrained Cody, who was glassy-eyed and screaming in terror. The nurses also helped to hold Cody down to immobilize her for the sutures. Fifteen minutes later the medical emergency was over.

The doctor told them that she expected the cut to heal well; there were no internal injuries. Cody was given a lollipop. The family returned home, exhausted, but relieved. This was the story that was conveyed to me by Joanna the next morning on the telephone. Medical healing had begun; emotional healing would take more time.

The following week Joanna, and Cody with a small Band-Aid on her forehead, returned to the mother-child group. Cody eagerly entered the playroom, hung her coat on her blue hook, and began to play with the dollhouse. She vigorously and repeatedly jumped the little girl doll on the small dollhouse sofa. Abruptly her play stopped. After a brief pause the play was repeated, and then repeated again, and again. She was unable to develop the play or to play with anything else. It seemed as though Cody had begun to use play to process the accident, but was unable to elaborate the play into a useful scenario. There was more to the story.

Joanna entered the mothers' room and almost threw herself onto the banquette with a sigh of despair. She told the other mothers the story of Cody's accident as she had told it to me earlier in the week on the phone. However, there were three additions.

First, every time Cody heard an ambulance siren since the accident, she began to scream uncontrollably. The screaming lasted about 20 minutes. The only thing that stopped her crying was a lollipop. The abrupt termination and rigid repetition of Cody's play jumping the doll on the sofa, combined with the lollipop to soothe her after hearing ambulance sirens, seemed to be her incomplete, fragmented memory of the accident. The jumping had preceded the accident and the lollipop was how it ended. The entire middle that included her mother's panic and shriek, the blood, the ambulance ride, being restrained, her pain, and her fear were missing. It suggested to me that Cody needed help to construct a more useful memory narrative about the accident that might enable her to elaborate her accident play and help her to adapt better. She needed her parents' help. More elements of the accident, including feelings, needed to be added.

Second, in Joanna's retelling the story of the accident to the mothers' group, her guilt and unremitting self-accusations for not having protected Cody enough to prevent the accident, and her self-recriminations for becoming overwhelmed, out of control, and initially immobilized, were gaining strength. Third, from Joanna's description it seemed that Stanley's coping style was the polar opposite of hers and the differences were straining recovery for the entire family.

Stanley focused on Cody's excellent medical outcome that helped him to tolerate his own guilt for having not been there and to withstand Joanna's rage. Joanna focused on the emotional pain including her panic at the time of the accident, Cody's terror, and all the what-could-have-beens and what-ifs. In addition, Joanna was perpetuating her emotional anguish and escalating anxiety with harsh self-accusations and rage at Stanley. As Cody's mother and father were caught in a spiraling cycle of guilt and rage, Cody was left alone in the aftermath of the accident.

I asked Joanna how she, Stanley, and Cody were talking together about what had occurred. According to Joanna, the only part of the accident included in the family's shared memory narrative was, "You got a booboo on your head, we went to the doctor, and got a lollipop." It seemed as though Cody needed ways to process with her parents more of the details of the accident. Joanna and Stanley needed help reconciling their different coping strategies so they could help Cody.

I met with Joanna and Stanley to talk about the accident, the differences in their coping styles, their anger toward each other, and Cody's need for help to think about the accident. Together we reviewed what had occurred and their feelings. I suggested ways of creating a shared memory narrative together with Cody. In addition to talking with Cody, they decided to make an illustrated book about the accident together.

The following week Joanna brought the picture book to the mothers' group. Joanna read the story. "Mommy and Cody were waiting for daddy to come home. Cody was having fun jumping on the sofa. Cody fell and bumped her head. There was a lot of blood." Joanna told us that Cody added, "Mommy was scared. Mommy cried." Joanna continued reading, "Cody and mommy went in the ambulance to see the doctor at the hospital. The ambulance siren was loud. Daddy ran fast and met them at the hospital. Mommy and the nurses held

Cody tight so she couldn't move. Cody cried. She was scared. Mommy cried. The doctor wore a mask; she put in the stitches and covered the boo-boo with a Band-Aid. Cody got a lollipop. Cody, mommy, and daddy went home. Cody got all better."

As Joanna told us about the writing of the book together, it seemed as if the book was as much for Joanna and Stanley as it was for Cody. Cody began to act out the co-created shared memory narrative in her pretend play.

At the beginning, Cody and her parents played hospital and read the book frequently. In a few days, Cody's crying when she heard an ambulance siren diminished and then stopped. They continued for a while to read the accident book and to play going to the hospital. Within a month, the accident play had stopped and the book was read on occasion.

Two possible reasons that Cody no longer cried when she heard ambulance sirens may have been time had passed since the accident, or she had forgotten about it. A more compelling explanation is that Cody stopped screaming when she heard ambulance sirens because she now had an organized memory narrative to help her to think about many elements of the accident together with her parents. She was no longer alone with her memories without words. She now had a shared memory narrative with her parents that included the emotionally charged specifics and feelings.

Parents are vulnerable to feeling guilty about their children. Joanna's extreme self-blame may have been connected to an accident that had occurred many years before she was born. Joanna's father's younger sister had died at 3 years of age in a car accident. Joanna's grandfather had been driving the car and spent the rest of his life overwhelmed by guilt. Joanna emphasized, "No one in the family blamed him, it was an accident, but he blamed himself." Joanna's self-blame, not only for Cody's recent accident but also for frequent minor accidents, was extreme. The intergenerational transmission of trauma related to accidents and guilt in Joanna's family needed to be understood better.

After a memory narrative is co-created with parents, children sometimes further their adaptation with their own pretend play. Savannah created her own imaginative play to consolidate, integrate, and further master the impact of an accident in her own unique way.

Savannah was 20 months old. While ice-skating with her family, her mother accidently stepped on her finger. Savannah's nail was ripped off. After an x-ray and several painful injections to numb her fingers, a bandage was applied in the E.R. that covered her entire hand for a week. There was uncertainty as to whether her nail would grow back. An elaborate shared memory narrative was created with her parents. After the bandage was removed, her finger was healing, and the nail was growing back, Savannah's main play activity for several weeks was shredding pieces of paper, crumpling the pieces together into a ball the same size as her bandaged hand had been, and binding the clump together with Scotch tape. This activity was repeated many times a day. The corner of her bedroom floor was piled high with these put-together body repair constructions. Savannah's play represented the accident, the medical treatment, and most importantly, the healing. The play had been entirely created by Savannah as a way to cope with the damage to her body. When her feeling of body integrity was restored, the play was no longer needed.

Children's play expresses a rich representation of their inner world. Understanding the meaning of a child's play helps parents to support the child's play, as occurred with Savannah. Parent-child memory narrative co-construction can provide the scaffolding for the child's own adaptive imaginative play.

Creating shared memory narratives can be difficult when parents' feelings interfere with the process. When the people who care for babies and young children quit or are fired, strong feelings erupt. Nannies, babysitters, and day-care staff who care for children become important figures in their emotional lives. When they leave, children grieve. Parents also establish bonds, sometimes with conflicted feelings, with their children's caregivers. They have entrusted the care of their children to them and rely on them. Parents have complex reactions when child-care helpers leave that sometimes merge with revived childhood memories of loss. The following story about Judy and Derrick after the nanny quit is an example.

Judy and Derrick "My nanny just quit . . ."

During a mothers' group that had been meeting for about 2 years, Judy announced that Nora, her 30-month-old son Derrick's nanny since his birth, had quit. Judy was angry and felt betrayed. Judy worked more than full-time and was totally dependent on child-care help. She had believed that Nora loved Derrick. "If that's how she really feels, I'm glad to be rid of her." When asked what she had said to Derrick about Nora leaving, Judy replied, "Nothing. Talking to Derrick will only make things worse. If he wanted to talk about her, he would." Furthermore, according to Judy, "There is nothing to talk about."

Since Nora had left, Derrick, who had been an easy, cooperative little boy, had become increasingly "difficult." His mother said that Derrick had become "demanding, oppositional, and crying all the time. He's impossible." Yet, Judy still refused to talk to him about his absent beloved nanny. Derrick began throwing things, hiding until his mother was screaming in desperation to find him, protesting even brief separations, and pooping in his underpants. It was easy for me to connect the specific behaviors Judy was describing to Derrick's grieving the loss of Nora and to his inability to organize his thoughts and feelings into words in order to adapt. The women in the mothers' group suggested to Judy that maybe Derrick's behavior was linked not only to his sadness about Nora leaving, but also to the fact that nothing had been said about it. Judy rejected this possibility vehemently. I stated, "It sounds like the thought of Derrick being sad about losing Nora is so painful to you that you need to deny that he cares or notices." I further said, "Maybe you are avoiding talking to Derrick about Nora because you think not talking about it is the right thing to do." I suggested what she might say to Derrick if she changed her mind.

The following week Nora told the group that Derrick's behavior had become "more difficult" and that he was refusing to go to nursery school. She said, "Three days ago when I was tucking Derrick into bed, I decided to talk to him about Nora. I had to try something; he was impossible." Judy told us about their conversation which was a version of what I had suggested. "I said to Derrick, I wonder what you are thinking about Nora and why she left. I guess you miss her. We haven't seen her for a long time. She doesn't work here anymore. It was a grown-up decision for her to leave. I guess you think about her sometimes. I probably should have said something sooner." Judy continued, "Derrick began to sob, I felt so terrible for him. For the first time he was crying in grief like a grown-up, not like a child wanting his own way." I said, "It sounds like you were able to tolerate Derrick's pain and that helped him." I wondered to myself what had been Judy's personal experiences of loss that she was not discussing, or even remembering.

The next day on the way to school, Derrick asked his mother if the scrape on Nora's knee was better. The last time Derrick had seen Nora, her knee was covered with a large bandage after a fall. The injury had occurred when Nora tripped over Derrick's fire truck that had been left in the hall. Derrick's mother reassured him, "Yes, her knee is all better." Derrick kissed his mother goodbye and ran into school.

Part of Derrick's reaction to Nora leaving seemed to have been his concern that she left because of her injury that had been caused by his fire truck. Derrick seemed to have been worried that it was his fault and that talking about Nora was not allowed. His mother talking to him about Nora opened the conversation and helped Derrick to ask about Nora's sore knee.

For a while, Derrick and his mom talked about Nora, the games they had played, and the books they had read together. Memories about the happy times they had shared were being co-constructed. At times they talked about Derrick's sadness and anger when Nora left, and his concerns about her tripping on his truck. Memories of love, loss, sadness, anger, and recovery were being created together. Derrick's "impossible, difficult behavior" ended. In a short while, they only talked about Nora on occasion.

A year later, some light was shed on Judy's reaction when Nora had left. One of the women in the group had a dog that died. Her dog was very old, sick, and in pain. She was describing how she, her husband, and their two children had a special goodbye before the dog was taken to the vet to be given an injection, only for dogs, when it is time for them to die. Judy recalled the loss of her own dog when she was a little girl. She remembered going to sleep-away camp for one month when she was 11 years old. When she returned home, her dog was not there. She was never told what happened, but remembered some of her thoughts. "I didn't know if she was hit by a car, ran away, or was given away. Nobody would talk to me about it. I guess last year when Nora left, this memory about my dog was influencing me not talking to Derrick, as my parents had not talked to me. I didn't think about it then." Judy's revived memory and her new insight about repeating with Derrick what her parents had done with her promoted her conviction about the importance of talking with children about events and creating shared memories.

Creating and revising shared memories with children is an ongoing process. Liliana was 6 years old and was visiting the Center with her grandmother. Liliana had attended playgroups when she was 1.5 years to 3 years old. As she was playing with the dollhouse, seemingly out of nowhere, she told her grandmother, "I remember when I was 2 years old you lied to me." Feeling horrified, Grandma responded, "I would never lie to you, I don't remember that happening." Liliana rebutted, "Yes you did, you lied, I remember." Grandma restated, "I can't imagine that I would ever lie to you. What do you remember I lied about?" Perhaps attempting to further engage her grandmother to remember the incident, Liliana suggested a less denigrating transgression and reconsidered her accusation. "Maybe it wasn't a lie. Maybe you tricked me." Grandma now had a vague recollection. Gently defending herself, while at the same time acknowledging the possibility that she had tricked Liliana, she said, "Maybe I was trying to get you to do something that you wouldn't do and I was so frustrated. I should not have tricked you." Neither Liliana nor Grandma could remember the details of the incident that had occurred. They both knew it feels bad to be tricked and to trick. Liliana appeared satisfied and remained thoughtful. I wondered to myself whether Liliana and her grandmother had arrived at a memory narrative that satisfied them both. I said, "People sometimes remember things differently. Talking about different memories of the same event can change memories and create new memories."

Liliana had been trying hard to do all the things her parents and teachers wanted. When she failed, she felt awful. Liliana's conversation with her grandmother was an opportunity to be forgiving to her grandmother, as she wished others would be with her. It also helped her to feel less self-critical, as she had observed her grandmother become less self-critical for a similar kind of transgression.

7 Parent-Child Differences

Just as all humans are unique, all parents are different from their children. Parents react to the differences: differences from themselves, from what they imagined, or from what they wished. Parent-child differences in physical traits and temperament characteristics are sometimes pleasurable and enriching, and sometimes disturbing.

When a child has a trait that is completely alien to a parent, a trait that a parent has but is trying to conceal or deny, or a trait that a parent envies, it may be difficult for the parent to identify with their child or to be empathic. In contrast, what appear to be extreme surface differences, disabilities, or anomalies to others can evoke parents' extraordinary identification. Some parents want to do everything possible to remove a birthmark. The blemish seems large and dwarfs other characteristics. For other parents, a birthmark or disability seems to disappear.

When a baby reminds a parent of a sibling rival or of their own parent rather than what they had imagined consciously or unconsciously, ghosts can create havoc. A mother who had an estranged relationship with her father told me, "I was unable to breastfeed because my baby looked just like my father. It was weird. I never thought my baby would look like my father." After her baby was born, her conflicts about how close to and how distant from her father she wanted to be had intensified and interfered with nursing.

Parents' reactions to hair color or texture can be triggered by their baby's hair. Recently, a mother told me about her struggle with her baby's red hair. Red hair was foreign to her, not of her. She asked rhetorically, "Where did she come from?" She was frequently asked by others, "Where did she come from?" By the time she had her fourth child with red hair, she identified her children as her own in part by the color of their hair. What had been alien became more than familiar. Red hair had become family.

The socialized veneer of assertiveness that adults acquire and hone can crumble when faced with the mean teasing, greed, or primitive physical aggression of little boys and girls. When parents are confronted with the as yet unsocialized aggressive behavior of children and deny their own aggressive feelings and impulses, they may view the typical behavior of children as dangerous or abnormal. Children use play to manage their aggressive impulses, thoughts, and feelings. Kicking a ball, punching a blow-up clown, dueling with soft swords, and a variety of water toys that squirt are forms of aggressive play. Pretend play may also have aggressive themes that are useful to children. If children's aggression makes parents feel uncomfortable about their own underlying aggression, they may be tempted to prohibit healthy forms of aggression that might benefit their children in play and in their social interactions.

Recently Bethany told me about her 2-and-a-half-year-old son, Otis. Bethany explained, "Other children are always taking toys away from him. He's a very sweet boy. He shares his toys all the time. He's generous and nice. I think he takes after me. He's not rough like my brother was when we were little. When Otis is playing with something and another child approaches him, he just hands the toy over. I used to think that was good. I don't know how to help him stand up for himself." I said, "It sounds like you and Otis are angry when children take toys away from him. Both you and Otis may be afraid of angry feelings. He needs to know it's ok to feel angry." Bethany looked curious. I continued, "You want Otis to be more assertive, but you don't want him to be an aggressive, hostile bully like you remember your brother. I wonder if it would help if together you played a kicking game or a dueling game with swords. Children need to feel entitled to defend themselves and empowered to assert themselves: these are healthy forms of aggression."

The following week Bethany and Otis entered the playroom with two long rubber swords. Bethany told me with delight that she and Otis were having fun dueling and that he had started asserting himself with other children. They were taking the swords everywhere with them. With his mother's support, Otis was holding on to toys and telling children who tried to take things away from him, "Stop. It's my turn." Bethany added, "I had wanted him to be a nice boy not a bully, but I was afraid to help him stand up for himself. Even that seemed too aggressive. We are both having fun with the swords." Otis being the same as his mother in terms of aggression was important to Bethany.

Gender differences between a parent and child can provide the parent with an opportunity for vicarious pleasure or evoke revived fear or envy. This can be particularly apparent during diaper changing and potty training. A father's avoidance of changing his daughter's diaper may be triggered by revived anxieties related to male-female genital differences or concerns about sexual arousal. A mother may share vicariously in her son's pride and pleasure in his penis or revived feelings of fear, envy, or inadequacy may be triggered.

Recently a mother told me about her two sons. She thought her older son had a big penis that she was proud of and her younger son had a little penis. Potty training with the older son went easily. The trouble she was having with her younger son seemed to be related to the denial of her devaluation of his penis that she thought was inadequate. An indication of this was her frequent repetition of, "It's not how big it is that matters, it's what you do with it." When he signaled his mother that he was about to urinate and wanted her to take him to the bathroom, she ignored him. I suggested, "It seems hard for you to imagine that he needs to make a big pee-pee urgently with such a little penis." I continued, "He thinks he has a powerful penis that is able to do wonderful things: it feels great to him." My vision of her son's penis – a penis to be proud of – helped her to take him to the potty before he urinated in his diaper. He was soon toilet trained.

In addition to the personal meanings of gender, economic and political gender inequalities and cultural attitudes toward gender play a role in parents' reactions to the gender of their children and gender-related attributes. Gender stereotypic physical traits, behavioral characteristics, and play preferences can trigger strong reactions in parents. A gender lens can color the meaning of a child's specific gait, gesture, preferences, or abilities. The gender meaning attached to the trait may shape the parents' response, which will then influence the child. An athletic father who has a non-athletic, artistic son may react not only to their differences, but also to the sexual orientation and gender identity implications he attaches to the trait.

Carla was in a mothers' group. She described herself as a woman who rejected female gender stereotypes and found her daughter's exclusive choice of sparkling party dresses and dolls disturbing. She did not want her daughter to be a "girly-girl." Carla and her almost 3-year-old daughter had repeated fights about what to wear and what to play with until Carla remembered that her own mother wanted her to be a different kind of girl than she wanted to be. Carla remembered that when she was a little girl her mother had wanted her to wear bows in her hair and uncomfortable dresses with tights and a dress coat. Now her mother wanted her to wear make-up. "My mom always says things like, get a hairstyle, dress more elegantly, you still look like a ragamuffin tomboy." With this awareness, Carla was able to allow her little girl to wear dresses; to be the kind of girl she wanted to be. In addition, she was able to enjoy her daughter's pleasure in being a girl even though the symbols her daughter chose were not the same as her own.

Parents' ghosts may also be activated when children have an attribute that is highly desired but unattainable by a parent. A nonmusical parent may envy the musical ability of a child. Envy can trigger vicarious pleasure and elicit parental pride and encouragement or may feel like losing a competition resulting in the parent's interference with the child's ability, interest, or trait.

When a child's risk-taking is unacceptable to a parent who is risk avoidant but who secretly wishes to be more adventurous, limit setting can be more challenging because not only is there parent-child conflict, but also internal conflict in the parent. Kelly refused to let her daughter, Keri, whom she knew was capable, climb to the top of the monkey bars until she remembered that when she was a little girl she had always wanted to do it but was too afraid.

Traits of introversion and extroversion often mobilize ghosts. A mother who characterized herself as shy and reserved described her 2-year-old daughter: "She's such a show-off. She's always trying to be the center of attention. I don't like it. I'm not like that." The mother's general reserved demeanor was different from her exuberant outgoing daughter's. In addition, her revived memories of her older sister whom she believed "did everything better" and "was always in the spotlight" had triggered a ferocious competition with her daughter that she felt she was losing. As she began to recognize that she had displaced feelings she had toward her sister onto her daughter, she became able to distinguish her painful childhood memories and continued rivalry with her sister, from the normal needs of 2-year-old children to be admired.

Cultural differences are sometimes linked to childhood memories and childrearing approaches. Painful memories may be dismissed as cultural differences and at the same time create internal conflict about childrearing approaches. Parents' feelings about loyalty to and betrayal of their own parents, or the meaning of being the same or different from their parents, may get denied or dismissed as cultural differences. For example, Adrian, who had been raised in Italy and whose parents were both Italian, described his parents' childrearing approach as "very Italian." This included being hit and forced to eat things he did not want. Describing the way he was raised in cultural terms rather than personal terms protected Adrian from being critical of his parents or angry with them, but also made it more difficult to resolve his own conflicts about how he wanted to raise his daughter.

In a sense there are both personal and cultural ghosts that may need to be disentangled. Rhonda talked about cultural differences between the United States and India, her family's country of origin. All disagreements she had with her parents, friends, and acquaintances were dismissed as cultural differences. "It's just the way it is. The two cultures are different." She was theoretically critical, but felt personally neutral toward her family and friends for the things they did that she considered "typical Indian."

Rhonda and her mother-in-law had not spoken for 5 years. Rhonda noted, "Since the fight, we never talk to each other in person or on the phone. My husband and the children see her twice a year and speak to her frequently. I never talk to her. Too many cultural differences."

After we had been meeting in a mother-child group for about a year and a half, for the first time Rhonda described the affectionate relationship she and her mother-in-law had before the fight that triggered their estrangement. "The fight changed everything; it was about what restaurant to eat at. I wanted American, she wanted Indian. Before the fight we liked each other." I remarked, "It sounds like you had a loving relationship before the fight." Rhonda sighed. I continued, "Your loving relationship was ruptured and has never been repaired." Rhonda then described the fight differently than she ever had before. She added, "I remember her face, she looked deranged, completely crazy. I don't remember her words; the sound is muffled. Her words are a blur." I said, "It sounds to me as if you are remembering being a terrified little girl confronted with a dangerous attack by a vicious adult." Rhonda went on, "Since our fight 5 years ago, I can't look her in the eye. I can't smile at her, I can't talk to her."

Rhonda's response was a confirmation of my understanding of a revived childhood memory: a ghost had intruded but was not remembered. Her statement suggested that when in her mother-in-law's presence, she experienced the same fear she had as a child. What she had dismissed as cultural differences and a fight about what restaurant to eat at, and I had understood as a rupture in a loving relationship, was now remembered by Rhonda as childhood terror and understood by me as reactivated trauma. Rhonda reflected, "Each time I see her I feel the fear." Rhonda's new understanding of her memory about the fight with her mother-in-law began to include memories of childhood fears. The estrangement from her mother-in-law began to heal.

Language differences can trigger ghosts. A parent's first language of childhood has deep-rooted meaning. Implicit and explicit childhood memories related to language are powerful. Sometimes a first language is preserved and is the primary language spoken to the baby; sometimes it is abandoned. Bilingual and trilingual families navigate the inclusion, exclusion, and exclusivity achievable through language. One language may predominate loving interactions and the other angry ones. When the primary language spoken at home is different from the community language, tensions around when to speak each may occur.

Camille spoke exclusively French to her 2-and-a-half-year-old daughter, Antoinette. When in English-speaking social situations with other children and adults, this created a bubble around Antoinette and Camille that interfered with Antoinette's developing social interactions with other children and adults. Camille recognized this, but was unable to integrate English into their interactions until she became aware of her sad feelings when she spoke English to Antoinette. Camille's mother lived in France and did not speak any English. Camille and I began to understand that when she spoke English to Antoinette, she felt not only far away from her mother, but also that she was excluding her mother. Speaking exclusively French to Antoinette helped her to feel closer to her mother and to Antoinette. This insight helped Camille expand Antoinette's social interactions. This was particularly important because Antoinette was going to start pre-school in several months.

Differences within families can become nodal points for conflict, both interpersonal and intra-psychic. Identifying related ghosts can be requisite for resolution. In the next story, the meaning of skin color differences to the mother had a disturbing impact on her relationship with her 20-month-old daughter.

Rose and Melanie
"I had the lightest skin in the family . . ."

Rose and her husband had lived in the United States since they were young children and had moved to New York City recently. Both of their families of origin were from Bangladesh. Rose was concerned about her 20-month-old daughter Melanie's development and called for a consultation.

I greeted Rose and Melanie at the door and led them past the slatted shutters and waiting room chairs into the toddler playroom. Rose followed me; Melanie entered behind her mother. I sat on the carpet in front of a toy shelf. Similar to her mother, Melanie was petite, with shoulder-length, soft, dark, curly hair, and coffee-colored skin. She was delicate and graceful. Rose chose to sit on a red cushion closest to the door and farthest away from the toys. Melanie entered, walked past her mother and past me to the other side of the room. As she circled the perimeter of the room, she picked up toys and threw them onto the floor. Before throwing each toy, she bit it. She bit hard and soft toys, plastic and wooden. Sometimes it was one hard bite and then she tossed it aside. Other times, Melanie repeatedly bit the toy and vigorously rubbed it against her gums, consuming her complete attention. The biting and flinging toys entirely replaced any play or interaction with her mother.

While Melanie darted around the playroom biting and tossing toys, Rose told me about the difficulties she had with Melanie since she was born. "She never cuddles with me. Sometimes she won't even look at me. It's been like this since she was born. She's so active, all over the place. She rubs toys in her mouth so vigorously, she gets frantic and can't stop. She's not talking; I'm worried."

Rose and Melanie did not interact with each other in any observable way. I wondered about how the physical and emotional distance between them was related to Melanie's biting. It was premature to explore this theme directly. I thought I could use play to bring Rose and Melanie closer, but they did not play together; Melanie did not play at all.

In order to attribute motivation and meaning to Melanie's behavior, I began by reformulating aspects of Rose's description of Melanie in relational terms. I commented, "When Melanie withdraws from you, she may need something from you. We don't know yet what it is, but we can work together to try to understand it." To Melanie I made comments attributing motivation and meaning to her biting. "You are a little girl, but you are strong. You are a strong biter. You can bite so many things." My thinking was that talking about the biting, describing it, and attributing meaning to it would change the experience of the biting for both Melanie and for her mother. Though it was unclear how or in what ways it would change, change was needed. Something was interfering with Rose and Melanie connecting and something was driving Melanie's throwing and biting. We agreed to meet together twice a week.

Over the next two weeks, I made comments to Rose and Melanie, highlighting and elaborating relationship themes. I began putting into words what I thought Melanie might be thinking about or wanting from me or from her mother. I made comments to Melanie in response to subtle communications. For example, when Melanie took a step in my direction but then turned away: "You don't know me yet, so you don't want to look at me or get too close." When she slightly glanced at her mother I said, "Mommy is watching you. Mommy and I are talking. Maybe you want us to play with you." I emphasized Rose's interest in Melanie: "Mommy is telling me so many things about you."

Responding to my interest in her and her mother's increased focus on her, Melanie began handing toys to me and then to her mother. This was an important turning point. We elaborated this into a game of handing toys back and forth to each other. "You give it to me, I give it to you. You give it to me, I give it to mommy, mommy gives it to you." We then played games of peek-a-boo and rolling a ball to each other. Within a few weeks, these self-other interaction games evolved into pretend mother-baby play with animals, and then with dolls. The pretend mother-baby play quickly became part of our usual play repertoire. Rose and Melanie amplified with pleasure any play that I started. Increasingly, Melanie and Rose played together while I watched. Melanie began to create her own mommy-baby play themes. She cuddled, fed, and put the dolls to sleep. Rose enthusiastically joined in. Through play, Melanie and Rose were interacting and building a relationship.

A world of play had opened up and was expanding fast. One day Melanie glanced at a banging toy. I took the opportunity to introduce aggressive play themes that I thought might help with her biting and throwing. With some encouragement, Melanie whacked the balls. At first Rose flinched. I commented to Melanie, "Oh, mommy got scared. You banged so loud and strong." Rose quickly joined us in the pleasure of Melanie's assertive, strong play. Rose's switch from startle to pleasure was important. It signaled that in the moment she felt safe with her own aggression and with Melanie's. Aggressive play was not a threat. Integrating aggressive themes into Melanie's play was age appropriate and seemed to have had some specific relevance to their relationship and to Melanie's biting.

Over the next several weeks as Melanie and Rose's play expanded to include both aggressive and typical care-taking mommy-baby themes, the biting and throwing toys began to diminish. Rose and Melanie became increasingly affectionate with each other. I decided to read *Mommy, Where Are You?* to them. With rapt attention, Melanie wanted me to read the book several times: she gleefully lifted the flap to find the hippo mommy. In the following weeks, each time we met Melanie gave the book to her mother to read. Rose told me, "I bought the book; we read it frequently at home. It's her favorite book."

Melanie's interest in *Mommy, Where Are You?* seemed beyond its general appeal to children almost 2 years old. On each page, the mommy is hidden behind a flap. The child opens the flap and finds the mommy. Melanie's repeated interest in *Mommy, Where Are You?* reinforced my thinking that in some ways Melanie had been struggling to find her mother. Rose's reading the book to Melanie and Melanie finding the mommy in the book mirrored what seemed to be occurring between them when we were together. In some ways, each time Melanie found her mother, she hid again. Each time we met, Rose and Melanie entered the playroom separately and gradually found each other again during our play. I did not yet know the reason. For now, I focused on promoting pleasurable, playful interactions between them and containing the aggression in play. We continued to read, *Mommy, Where Are You?*

Melanie had completely stopped throwing and biting toys. She was now able to play. Her pretend play was increasing, and her use of language was expanding. Rather than withdraw, Melanie initiated interactions with her mother. She sat on her lap, cuddled, and initiated play. We had created a playground in which ghosts could enter safely and be understood.

We had been seeing each other for three months. Rose began to talk about the "tension" with her own parents when she was a child and the difficulties she had. A turning point occurred when at the end of a session she told me, "I was the only dark-skinned child in an all-white school." Rose's ghosts had arrived.

The next day we met, Rose entered the playroom and commented, "I looked around Melanie's class yesterday and was struck that Melanie is the only dark child and I'm the only dark mom." Rose's comment about comparisons of skin color focused my attention on the difference between Melanie and Rose's skin colors. To my eye, Melanie was slightly darker than her mother. I had not appreciated what this might mean to Rose and how the difference in their skin color might have been affecting her, or both of them.

Rose began to tell me about skin color in her family of origin. Her father was the darkest, then her older brother, next was her mother, and then her two sisters. Rose was the lightest. According to Rose, she and her husband were the same color.

Rose had attributed certain advantages and successes in her life to her lighter skin. One night when Rose was a teenager, she and her girlfriends were trying to enter a club. The boys were already inside. The bouncer at the door waved Rose in. Her friends were not admitted. Rose told me as she cast her eyes down and lowered her voice, "The only reason I got in was because I passed for white, or white enough." The shame and guilt she felt for leaving her friends, and the rage she felt for the advantage she had because of lighter skin, were painful.

Up until this time, I had not realized that the closer Rose got to Melanie the darker she felt, and that this had been intolerable. When Rose walked down the street herself, she felt she passed for white but when she walked down the street with Melanie, she believed she did not. This was a revival of many childhood memories, day-to-day experiences in her current life, and a reason for distancing herself from Melanie. While Melanie sat on Rose's lap, I shared these thoughts with Rose and Melanie. Rose seemed to feel deeply understood. Melanie rested her head on her mother's breast. Rose held her close and gently caressed her hair. Rose confided, "I never thought of that. Sometimes I think about things even when I don't know it." I thought to myself that Rose's comment affirmed my statement about distancing herself from Melanie. The impact of my statement was reflected in the moment by Melanie and Rose's affectionate embrace. Rose then added, "Melanie is so agitated today." I noted, "You seem agitated and distracted too." Rose reflected, "I am. Maybe it's me whose agitated, maybe I see Melanie the way I feel. In certain situations I'm not available to her. When I'm embarrassed or worried, I withdraw." Rose's insight was profound. On the surface Rose was talking about being agitated. I understood her to also be describing her feelings related to skin color. What I heard was, when I see Melanie's skin as dark, it makes me feel dark; I get agitated. I then feel embarrassed and worried, and I withdraw.

We continued to meet for two more months. At the end of this time, much had changed. Melanie and Rose enjoyed pleasurable interactions. They were physically affectionate and played together. Melanie no longer threw or bit toys. Her play was now age appropriate, well organized, and sustained. Her language was developing. *Mommy, Where Are You?* was no longer the book they read most frequently. At our last session, when we were saying goodbye, Rose reflected, "When Melanie could find me, she found herself." I think Rose's statement also meant, when I found a part of myself that I had rejected, I found Melanie.

While there was more for Rose to understand about herself, her relationship with Melanie was now gratifying to her and nurturing to Melanie. This transformation in their relationship, Melanie's resumed development, and Rose's accompanying insight were achieved primarily through play.

Picture books create a special kind of play. They provide additional access to the inner world of children and the interpersonal world of parents and children. For Melanie and Rose (p. 103), *Mommy, Where Are You?* was a core theme.

Picture books are so frequently read and re-read because their themes are not only important in early development, but are relevant throughout life: *The Runaway Bunny*, *Caps for Sale*, *The Very Hungry Caterpillar*, and *The Kissing Hand*. The shared parent-child attention to these themes is enriching for both.

Inherent to the experience of reading books with young children is a shared focus of attention to mentally representing events and feelings in contrast to living them. The parent and child together reflect on the events and empathize with the characters. There is some distance from the intensity and stress that occur while living the same theme. When Melanie was struggling to find her mother in actuality, while reading *Mommy, Where Are You?* she always could find the mommy under the flap. Melanie finding mommy repeatedly was reliable and Melanie's mother repeatedly could enjoy the pleasure of being found. Skin color differences remained in the background.

Reading picture books to babies and young children activates the inner worlds of both the parent and the child together. The joint pleasure of this shared inner experience is compelling. For Rose and Melanie, who were trying to find each other, reading *Mommy, Where Are You?* was captivating. Once they found each other, the book had a different meaning to them.

8 Treasured Toys

Soft, brown teddy bears with shiny noses, pink bunnies with silk-lined ears, white fluffy kittens with tickling whiskers, and plush satin blankets are among the treasured toys of babies and young children.

Attachments to soft cuddly toys, blankets, and pillows create a special kind of play and reveal important aspects of babies' and young children's developing minds (described by Donald Winnicott as transitional objects). The toy may have been introduced by parents and have objective qualities that make it appealing, but the baby or toddler creates the meaning of the treasured toy. It may have always accompanied feedings since infancy or been among many toys huddled on a shelf and claimed by a toddler. Either way, the intensity of a toddler's growing attachment to a lovey, what it comes to mean to the child, including its power to soothe, comes from the child's mind. It is a developmental achievement.

The treasured toy may be a frequent companion or be exclusively a valued sleep partner. Even if parents have created obstacles to its access, it remains itself available. It is never angry, sad, or busy. Its ability to soothe remains constant. It can be thrown or ignored by the child, and is always there to be reclaimed. This is all achieved by the child's mind. Parents help to protect it and to care for it. Its importance to the child is recognized. Treasured toys often have a name that has been co-created by a parent and child together.

External features of the treasured toy change because it has been cuddled, dragged, sucked, dirtied, and washed. And while it looks bedraggled and threadbare with missing limbs and other parts to the rest of the world, it is more highly valued by the child than ever. The child has endowed it with personal meaning that will persist until it is no longer needed because the child's mind has developed and can perform the needed functions without the treasured toy: maintain a positive sense of self, tolerate frustration, self-soothe, tolerate ambivalent feelings, and regulate emotions.

It is common for childhood treasured toys to have been kept into adulthood. Special toys and treasured blankets, dolls, and stuffed animals are carefully stored in memory trunks, tucked far away at the back of closets, or strewn around attics. Some remain in childhood bedrooms long abandoned, maybe seen on occasion. Others are kept near. These treasured items are frequently known by the next generation. Sometimes, the next generation acquires them.

Before Eric was born, his mother bought a soft, silky-white baby-comforter for him. When she nursed him, she kept it close. When she settled him on the floor to play, the blanket was under him. When the family traveled, they took it with them. When Eric began to walk, he dragged the blanket from room to room and took it with him whenever he left the apartment. When he cried, he soothed himself cuddling with Blanky.

When Eric was 3 years old, he no longer used Blanky for soothing, companionship, or play. The blanket was now faded and threadbare. Its stuffing was coming out. It had been well loved and was no longer needed. Eric had used it well. He no longer needed it to serve the psychological functions it had served before. Eric was an emotionally well-regulated, confident, and competent little boy. Eric's mother stored the blanket in her linen closet.

Eric grew up and got married. When his baby son Drake was born, Eric asked his mother for the blanket. While he had not seen it for years, he was sure that his mother still had it. Eric's mother-in-law re-fabricated Blanky into a quilt for Drake. The tattered segments were discarded. The new Blanky became Drake's treasured toy. When Drake was 8 years old, he noted, "The most important thing to me about my blanket is that it was my dad's." Blanky is now in Eric's linen closet and contains an intergenerational transfer of meaning.

Children who don't have a treasured toy have other play that serves the same function. Some babies and toddlers make humming noises, repeat a word, or sing a song before falling asleep, when separated from their mothers, or for soothing at other times. A mother recently told me that ever since she can remember, she falls asleep imagining the rhythm of her mother's heartbeat as she first did when she was a child.

When I started telling friends and colleagues that I was writing a book about childhood memories, they frequently told me about their teddy bears, bunnies, blankets, and other treasured toys. I discovered that some of the most vivid, cherished childhood memories are about treasured objects. Both the loving comforting memories and the emotionally painful haunting memories about treasured toys were eagerly recounted. One thing shared by all the stories was the enduring importance of the memories. Each story about a treasured toy was told with passion.

From the treasured toy stories I have collected, I arrived at a new understanding. Adult memories of treasured toys continue to serve functions similar to the treasured toys of childhood. When they are recalled, comfort and pleasure are evoked. Even when the memories include a treasured toy's abrupt loss, or the toy was treasured in the context of threatening and difficult childhood experiences, the pleasurable memory of the object remains and tempers the surrounding pain.

A father of two little girls recently told me that his own baby blanket is kept in a closet in his mother's apartment. He had not seen it for years. He said, "I never think about it, but if I held it, I know I would have a special feeling."

Following are excerpts from the collection of treasured toy stories told to me by colleagues and friends.

Patrick
"Three generations of lost Bunnies . . ."

As I finished telling Patrick about writing *Parenting and Childhood Memories*, he told me, through intermittent tears, his story about three generations of lost bunnies: his own, his daughter's, and his granddaughter's.

When Patrick was a young boy, he had a treasured stuffed animal. Its name was Bunny. Bunny was very soft. It was light brown, with a shiny black nose, sparkling eyes, and long floppy ears. It was perfect for cuddling. Patrick always kept Bunny close. He pushed Bunny in the playground swing, pulled it in his red wagon, and slept with Bunny every night. Most importantly when Patrick was sad, angry, or felt any kind of pain, physical or emotional, he soothed himself with Bunny. During each year, Bunny became softer, dirtier, and acquired a unique texture and familiar scent. Bunny was well loved.

Patrick had severe allergies. Because of his allergies, Patrick's mother thought it prudent to discard Bunny each year on his birthday. Patrick was required to place Bunny into a "shoebox coffin" and throw it into the incinerator. Patrick's eyes filled with tears as he recounted these details. Bunny was replaced each year with a clean, new Bunny. This annual birthday ritual was repeated for many years. Each year Patrick grew to love the new Bunny. However, the sadness of the loss each year remained and compounded. His view of his mother as hurtful and unfeeling grew exponentially. His love for Bunny grew and grew with each new Bunny.

When Patrick was 8 years old and visited his grandmother who lived down the block for a sleepover, he left Bunny at home. He wept for his mother to bring Bunny to him. She refused. The sadness, anger, and helplessness of being required to throw Bunny into the incinerator each year was reinforced and consolidated. His view of his mother as uncaring intensified.

When Patrick was 10 years old, Bunny was replaced with a new one for the last time. His allergies had subsided and Patrick was allowed to keep this Bunny. Patrick also started a collection of stuffed animals. A menagerie populated his bedroom.

When Patrick grew up and got married, his wife persuaded him to travel to Paris for their honeymoon. Separations and travel were not easy for Patrick. He was reluctant to leave home, but agreed to the romantic vacation. His allergies worsened in Paris. He was convinced it was the down feather-pillow on the hotel bed that was aggravating them. He called his mother in New York to FedEx his own non-allergenic pillow. This time, his mother sent his pillow: Patrick's allergy attack subsided.

Several years later, when Patrick's daughter was born, he eagerly gave a Bunny to her. For several months it sat in the corner of her crib. When she was about 10 months old she claimed it as her own. Patrick and his daughter played many games with Bunny and the large collection of stuffed animals he had created over the years. In their play, Patrick often spoke for Bunny. He noted this several times as we talked. Patrick did not elaborate on the significance of this part of his story. I wondered whether as Patrick gave voice to Bunny's thoughts and feelings in play with his daughter, he was no longer alone with his own thoughts and feelings as he had been as a child.

Patrick's daughter began to take Bunny everywhere. She also began to sleep with Bunny. Then a bad thing happened. While the family was vacationing, her Bunny was lost. Patrick and his daughter were grief stricken. For Patrick it triggered the repeated loss of his childhood Bunny each year on his birthday. For his daughter it was the first significant loss. Patrick recounted in detail, "I searched the hotel room, lobby, and playroom. I sifted through baskets of hotel laundry." Patrick emphasized, "Everyone except my mother understands what it means to a child to lose a Bunny." Bunny could not be found.

After two days and almost giving up ever seeing Bunny again, Bunny was found hidden in a suitcase. Through tears of joy, Bunny and the family were reunited. Patrick and his daughter were ecstatic.

Now an adult and a mother herself, when Patrick's daughter recalls losing Bunny when she was a little girl, the most important part of the memory for her is the depth of her father's shared sadness when Bunny was lost, his boundless efforts to find Bunny, and their shared joy when Bunny was found. For Patrick, sharing his daughter's grief and recognizing the importance to her of his empathy enabled him to understand that even more painful than losing his Bunny each year as a child had been the hopelessness and aloneness he felt when his painful feelings were not recognized, acknowledged, or accepted.

Patrick's daughter grew up and Patrick's 4-year-old granddaughter also had a treasured Bunny. Her Bunny was also lost. However, her Bunny was never found. Her mother and grandfather helped her to mourn Bunny. They talked about her sad feelings and missing Bunny. They remembered together the fun she had with Bunny. Sharing her grief, recognizing and accepting her feelings, Patrick was able to mourn with his daughter and granddaughter.

When Patrick's granddaughter was 7 years old, she formed a new, different kind of attachment to a toy. One of her dolls became her favorite doll. This special doll had the most outfits, was the doll most frequently dressed and re-dressed, and hair most frequently styled. It was not cuddled or slept with. It was not the same as her attachment to Bunny. A favorite doll of an older child has some remnants of the attachment of a younger child to a treasured toy, but it is different.

While Patrick was telling his Bunny stories to me, stories he had told many times before about events that had occurred during the past 70 years, he had a new insight. With amazement he told me that he just realized that his pillow that his mother had sent to him in Paris was a grown-up version of Bunny. Patrick's memories throughout his life of his mother's painful unresponsiveness to his needs for Bunny expanded to include a moment of her empathy. Memories continue to evolve and get reconstructed with self-reflection and insight.

Owen
"He's had his bunny for 16 years . . ."

Leslie recently told me about Dandy: a stuffed brown bunny that was given to her son Owen when he was born. "He's had his bunny for 16 years. He's still attached to it."

By the time he was 18 months old, Owen carried Dandy with him everywhere. Dandy sat next to him for meals, went to daycare with him, and was cuddled close while he slept. When Owen cuddled Dandy, he gently and rhythmically rubbed Dandy's ear against his upper lip, next to his nose. His mother could hear soft, sniffing sounds. Dandy was well love-worn, with a distinctive Dandy scent.

When Owen was 3 years old, Leslie and Owen's father took him on a vacation to Animal Kingdom. Dandy came with them. Owen's mother and father had decided to divorce. The family trip was planned in an effort to lessen the impact of the divorce on them all. After the vacation, when they arrived home, Dandy could not be found. He was lost. With no hope of ever finding Dandy, Leslie decided to replace Dandy with a new one that looked exactly the same; it would take a few days to arrive. Owen was told that Dandy was still at Animal Kingdom where he would be fed and washed, have fun with the other animals, and would be home in a few days. When the new Dandy arrived, there was much celebration. Owen quickly resumed his previous activities with Dandy. Owen now claims to have always known it was a new Dandy.

Owen's mother and father divorced as planned. Owen lived with his mother and frequently visited his father. He kept Dandy with him when he was in each parent's home. Owen adapted well to his parents' divorce.

Six years later, when Owen was 9 years old, there was a tragedy in the family. Owen's father had a massive heart attack and died. With the support of his mother and a large extended family, Owen coped with this profound loss. He resumed sleeping with Dandy.

Owen is now 16 years old. He does well in school, has a part-time after school job, and has his first girlfriend. He still has Dandy, who mostly remains on a shelf in his room. Sometimes on a rainy day as he reads on the living room sofa, he holds Dandy by the ear, and seemingly absentmindedly rubs the bunny against his upper lip. Again, Leslie can hear gentle sniffing sounds. It is easy to wonder about a connection for Owen between Dandy and daddy. While this is an unusual lovey bunny story, it is unusual for your father to die when you are 9 years old.

A few months after Leslie told me about Dandy, the family dog chewed and severed Dandy's paw. Owen asked his mother to repair Dandy, which she did. A week later Owen left Dandy on the floor and the dog got Dandy again. This time Dandy was damaged beyond repair. Dandy was in shredded pieces with clumps of stuffing scattered on the kitchen counter. Leslie told Owen, "Maybe it's time for a funeral." Although Owen had left Dandy in harm's way again, Owen said, "Definitely not."

Leslie's impulse again was to replace Dandy with a new one as she had done when Owen was 3 years old. After a long search, she found one on eBay and planned to give it to Owen for Christmas. Thinking that Owen may need help or even permission from his mother to relegate Dandy to a different place in actuality and his mind, I raised the possibility that while Owen did not want a funeral, he may be ready for Dandy to be more in the background and he may need help from his mother. I suggested, "Perhaps keeping Dandy's fragmented remains in a special box on a shelf in his room or in a closet would feel right." Leslie was delighted with this idea for Owen, but said it felt too sad for her. I wondered with her, "If you decide not to give Owen the new Dandy now, maybe you could give it to him when he grows up and has a baby." In the moment, Leslie seemed delighted with this idea. However, a week later she told me that while Owen had liked the idea of keeping Dandy for his future baby, it was too sad for her. Leslie was not ready for Dandy to be gone. For now, Dandy remnants and the new Dandy remain in Owen's room, on a high shelf, behind his books.

Helen
"My lifeline was thrown overboard . . ."

Helen began her story about her treasured jump rope by telling a life-long, recurring dream: "I'm running down the street being chased by a rat. I run into my house for safety, but it has no walls."

Helen was born in Israel. When she was 2-and-a-half years old, her mother died suddenly from an aneurysm. Her father temporarily put Helen into an orphanage until he could care for her himself. Almost one year later, when Helen got lice and her beautiful long blond curls were shaved off, her father took her out of the orphanage. Together they moved into a one-room apartment with a friend of his and her three children. Helen remembered, "She was like a mother to me. She gave me a braided jump-rope. I played with it all the time. It was my favorite toy. It wasn't a teddy bear or blanket, but in some ways it was."

When Helen was 5-and-a-half years old, her father remarried a woman Helen did not know. His new wife had already moved from Israel to New York where he planned to join her. Helen needed to leave the woman whom she thought of as her mother and the children whom she thought of as siblings. "Before I was 7 years old I had lost two mothers and was about to get a wicked step-mother."

Helen was allowed to choose one item to bring with her to New York. She chose her treasured braided jump-rope. Helen and her father traveled from Israel by ship in steerage. The men and women were separated. Clinging to her jump-rope, Helen was alone and terrified. Days later, as the ship approached New York, she and her father stood on deck. He took her jump-rope out of her hands and then told her, "We will have a new life in New York. Everything will be new." He then hurled Helen's jump-rope overboard.

I asked Helen what impact she thought these childhood memories have had on her life. She was clear. "Family is most important to me. When my son was little, I was very protective. I am very close to him and to my grandchildren. My lifeline may have been thrown overboard, but I am a survivor." After a brief pause she added, "My father survived Auschwitz."

The parallels between Helen's lifelong recurring dream and her memory of her treasured jump-rope are noteworthy. In her dream, the safety provided by house walls is absent. In her memory, the feelings of safety provided by her jump-rope are thrown overboard. Keeping her family close now provides feelings of safety. Intergenerational transfer of trauma is central to Helen's story.

Tony
"I do everything different with my children . . ."

Tony did not have a typical treasured toy when he was a child; however, in some ways, sumptuous Italian meals, with the freshest vegetables and aromatic sauces, were his.

Tony moved from a small town in Italy to the United States when he was a young man. He assured me that "New York City, my wife, my work, and how I raise my three daughters are completely different in every way from my life in Italy." While Tony's adult life is different from his childhood in most ways, in one way it is similar. With family recipes passed down from one generation to the next, Tony prepares meals created with the freshest ingredients. His favorite foods, prepared with love for friends and family, serve a similar function as the memory of a childhood treasured toy does for many adults.

While talking to me about the stuffed teddy bears that still remain on the beds of his three adult daughters, Tony recalled two vivid childhood memories. "When I was a little boy, every summer I went to stay with my grandmother for two months. My grandmother was a wonderful woman. Her house was huge. One morning she left the house early while I was still sleeping. She always went to the garden to pick the ripest, most luscious vegetables after the morning dew had softened their prickly exteriors. When I awoke, I searched the entire house and couldn't find her. I went from room to room crying. I went out on the enormous terrace screaming for her. I cried and cried, I remember it as though it were yesterday. After what seemed like a long time, still far away, I saw my grandmother walking toward the house carrying a basket-full of perfect vegetables to cook soups, sauces, and stews."

Tony's memory of the enormous size of the house and terrace highlights how small and frightened he felt left alone; his screams unheard. His memory also vividly includes his grandmother approaching from a distance with beautiful vegetables, freshly picked from the garden to cook into the wonderful meals he remembers. Tony notes that the vegetables' "prickly exterior is softened by the morning dew." Shadow memories of love, care, and safety, though far away, beneath the painful surface, and bathed by tears are included in his frightening memory.

Tony's second memory was about being locked in the attic by his mother. He described the dark, musty, rat-infested attic. He added that he was hit repeatedly and frequently, and then locked in the attic. "That's just the way it was. I was hit all the time. All the kids were."

Tony emphasized both the painful, frightening, and lonely parts of his childhood memories and how differently he was raising his own children. "I have never treated them the way I was treated. My wife and I talk to them about everything. I have never hit them. I support them. Everything was different in our town in Italy; it was a long time ago." As Tony highlighted the terror and pain of his childhood memories and distanced himself from his past, I had another thought. The raw vegetables from the far away garden carried by his grandmother approaching the house and rescuing him from the terror and aloneness he felt represent the love, pleasure, and care that Tony brought with him from Italy. This nurturing part of his memory is imbedded in the frightening part and is reflected in how Tony cares for his children and the meals he prepares with family recipes enriched with his own innovations. Tony's memories support the idea that Tony brought with him from childhood the raw ingredients for the loving relationships he has now with his wife and three daughters.

Mabel
"My parents bought me an imposter bunny . . ."

Mabel was 15 years old. As we sat talking about *Parenting and Childhood Memories*, she told me about her treasured toy. "I have had Bunny since I was a baby. When I was about 4 years old, I found another bunny tucked away in my mother's bedroom drawer. I couldn't believe it. I was standing there holding Bunny and there was another one that looked exactly the same. It was so weird. I couldn't figure it out. It was an imposter Bunny. How could there be two? Even now it still feels strange when I talk about it. My mother told me she bought it in case Bunny got lost. I was enraged at her, furious. I didn't want it, so she gave it to my baby brother."

As I listened to Mabel's story about her Bunny, I wondered about the connection between her feelings about the "imposter" bunny and her feelings about her new baby brother. I said, "In your memory, your parents wanted you to have two bunnies. Your parents now had two children." Mabel replied, "Wow, maybe my memory about the 'imposter' bunny and my anger at my mother is also about the birth of my brother." The meaning of Mabel's memory was expanding.

Gwen
"My mother took my special doll away . . ."

Gwen is now 45 years old. When she was 14 years old her mother took away her special doll. Gwen emphasized, "The only part of my doll that I remember is its arm. It's so strange, but that's the only part I remember." (Illustrating with her fingers, Gwen indicated that the doll's arm was about 7 inches long with about a 2-inch diameter.) "I always fell asleep with it pressed against my upper lip, right under my nose so I could smell it while sucking my fingers. I was so angry at my mother when she took it away. I don't know why she took it away. Even now when I can't sleep, I still think that if I had the doll, I would be able to fall asleep. I try to suck my fingers the same way, but it doesn't work without the doll." As Gwen talked, she gestured with her hands, fingers, and lips. She rubbed her nose back and forth vigorously with her finger trying to demonstrate and recreate the experience. She illustrated again the exact dimensions of the doll's arm.

I had some additional thoughts about Gwen's memory and the way she was telling it. I said, "In some ways, the way you are talking about your doll memories reminds me of masturbation." Gwen lit up and said, "In my home we never talked about sex. Masturbation would not be ok." I asked Gwen, "Why did your mother take your doll away?" Gwen did not know why, but seemed intrigued with the possible meanings of her memories. I wondered to myself whether Gwen's memory was about a prohibition of masturbation.

Jocelyn
"My treasured doll is not bequeathed . . ."

Sometimes treasured toys from childhood are kept close throughout life. Jocelyn had recently completed her will, probably for the last time. She was 98 years old and her first great-grandchild had just been born. As Jocelyn and I sat by the fire, basking in its warm glow and reminiscing, she told me about a moment's reflection while writing her last will and testament. She had included a few pieces of jewelry and several small silver items she had inherited from her mother, who had inherited them from her mother. Special books were also included. One important item did not fit into any of these categories – her treasured childhood doll with its bandaged, broken legs, since her sister threw it down the stairs when they were little girls. Jocelyn knew that it was the meaning of her doll to her as a child and the treasured memories of it throughout her life that were of value. She mused: still vivid near the end of life, the meaning of her doll would die with her.

9 Being Grandparents

Parenthood provides a unique opportunity for self-reflection, adult development, and new resolutions of long-standing interpersonal and intrapsychic difficulties, conflicts, and unresolved trauma. Being a grandparent provides another opportunity. Both childhood memories and memories of being a parent of young children can be reconfigured. Ghosts that were more intrusive when first becoming a parent, but were reshaped or became more porous throughout the passing years of parenthood, often have become somewhat vaporized when a grandparent.

Grandparents have the occasion to repair enduring vestiges of ruptures with their adult children and to form deeply satisfying relationships with their grandchildren. When grandparents look at their grandchild, they may see vivid reflections of themselves: times long past, self-states, and images profoundly pleasurable to recall. In many ways, this is the potential ongoing intergenerational magic of parenthood.

Grandparents have weathered the storms of having been young parents with babies and little children, learned through the middle school years, and traversed the turbulence of teenagers. While re-living those years again with their adult children and grandchildren, new experiences are possible and new memories created.

There is added magic accorded grandparents that is derived from their new position. Grandparents are close to their grandchildren, but not responsible for them. They take care of them, but not all the time. They teach them, but are less identified than parents with their failings. Parents benefit from grandparents' support and admiration, but do not require it. Grandparents' wisdom is welcomed, if not imposed. Their advice is sought, if not tinged with criticism. Access to grandchildren is offered, if not demanded. Parents thrive on the adoring love grandparents bestow upon their grandchildren and vicariously experience it.

Granny was visiting 10-month-old Arianna as she did weekly. Granny saw her frequently, but due to physical disability was unable to carry, bathe, or play with her on the floor. She had never given Arianna a bottle because she was being breastfed. When Arianna was an infant, she frequently played with Granny's necklace while sitting on her lap. Granny had rarely been able to hold her since. It felt to Granny that Arianna barely knew her; they needed a new personal game.

When Granny entered the house, Arianna was playing on the floor. Granny sat on the sofa, placed her purse next to Arianna, opened the intricate latch and invited Arianna to look inside. Arianna watched carefully as Granny showed her how to unzip the makeup case. Together, Arianna and Granny took out every item from the purse and the makeup case, and re-filled them again and again. This game intrigued Arianna and pleased Granny. The next time Granny came to visit, and the next time, and the next, Arianna excitedly looked for her purse. Together they played. Granny taught Arianna to open the purse and unzip the makeup case. They removed each personal item and sampled them one by one. Arianna had touched Granny's toothbrush, toothpaste, and lipstick. She had jingled her keys and emptied her wallet. They had established a special, intimate game. Granny felt known.

Arianna is now 8 years old and has developed a close relationship with Granny; she still enjoys looking through Granny's purse and especially her makeup case. She frequently tries on Granny's lip-gloss.

Granny has five grandchildren and they all are interested in the contents of her purse. In some ways their continuing fascination with the interior of her purse and the contents it holds mirrors Granny's fascination with their inner worlds.

Letter to My Grandchildren

June 2018

Dear Kaia, Isaac, Violet, Clio, and Evelyn, my precious grandchildren: this book was inspired by your parents and written for you. It will have different meaning to you when you read it as children, young adults, parents, and grandparents: meanings change.

Parenting and Childhood Memories is about parents, babies, and little children. It is filled with stories about ghosts, magic, and childhood memories that slip through time and crystalize when children grow up and become parents. The memories are happy and sad: loving, angry, frightening, and protective. Some memories are passed down from one generation to the next. When you become parents, your own childhood memories will be called to mind, as were those of your parents and grandparents.

The magic is the power of love and attachment. It enables parents to kiss their babies' pain and the tears vanish. The ghosts are remnants of past relationships. They are disguised in your nighttime dreams and invisible in the glare of sunlight. Your private thoughts and wishes are clues. Listen to the rhythm of your heartbeat.

Searching for shiny rocks hidden in our courtyard garden has been an exciting childhood adventure, with stumbles and unexpected treasures. Personal insight is a lifetime magical treasure hunt that reveals the gems of self-discovery.

While writing, I was surrounded by your photos and frequently gazed at them for insight. Memories of each of you and your parents are disguised and included in these stories. Perhaps you have found them.

Have fun. Much love always, Nana/Grandma

Epilogue

It has been a privilege to work with the parents and children who participated in Sackler Lefcourt Center programs throughout the last 37 years. While the stories in *Parenting and Childhood Memories* originated during Center mother-child groups and parent consultations, they are fictionalized versions of the actual parents and children.

The parents who join Center programs are highly educated and economically advantaged. They are typical in that they want the best for their children and want to be the best parents that they can be. They care about all aspects of their children: physical, emotional, social, and cognitive. They are ready to enter into supportive relationships that stimulate their curiosity about their child's developing mind and that heighten their own self-reflection. They are eager to learn about child development, the inner world of their children, and their own personal motivation for the childrearing decisions they make. They are curious about the ways in which their childhood memories influence their interactions with their children. They enjoy the pleasures of having young children and tackle the challenges with intelligence, open mindedness, and love. They are aware of their restless ghosts and have demonstrated how mother-baby and father-baby love can help to heal the scars left by their own childhood emotional pain. The children are also typical. Like their parents, their development is robust; they stumble at times and are resilient.

Center programs are an application of psychoanalytic theory and technique to early development and parenting. In mother-child groups while children play close to their mothers with the supervision of playgroup leaders, a wide range of child development and childrearing topics are discussed. Mothers' childhood memories are explored. Conscious and unconscious meanings are considered. The pleasures and stresses of having babies and young children are shared. The day-to-day typical problems and the unusual more difficult ones are processed together. Birthdays are celebrated. Developmental achievements are applauded. When accidents, illness, and troubles arise, empathy and support are provided. For many women, reflecting on early development in mothers' groups lessens the stress and increases the pleasure of raising young children. Developmental consultations for parents provide more focused, short-term attention to an emerging question or concern. The stories in this book originated during both parent consultations and mother-child groups.

Parents' courage and trust to share their childhood memories, to confront their ghosts, and the changes that followed provided the framework for this book. Each story shows the unique power of parent-child attachment and love. Parents have enormous influence on their children and at the same time the impact of babies and young children on their parents to motivate them to seek and to achieve personal insight is monumental.

For over 35 years I have talked with parents and together we have watched their babies develop. I have witnessed how the pleasurable and stressful events of their lives get constructed into shared memory narratives: memories that will include the ghosts of the children's futures. Some of those children are now parents returning to the Center with their own babies. For me, it has been an incredible journey. I am deeply indebted to all the parents and children throughout the years at the Center. They have been my most influential teachers.

The world-wide coronavirus erupted in the United States in February 2020. As I completed writing *Parenting and Childhood Memories*, there were enormous everyday life changes: uncertainty, illness, and many deaths. Schools and playgrounds closed, social distancing was observed, in many hospitals spouses were not permitted in delivery rooms, visitors were omitted from NICUs, and in some cities newborns were separated from their mothers. With all of this devastation, the psychological wellbeing of thriving young children seemed to be maintained. While the children were aware of changes in their surroundings and were impacted by the stress that their parents were experiencing, they continued to have joyful moments with their parents. The children's sense of a tomorrow and a "when I grow up" was sustained. Even during this unprecedented time of uncertainty, the joy reflected in a baby's smile and the glee emanating from a child's play revealed glimmerings of the future.

It is too soon to reflect on the impact the coronavirus outbreak will have on children and their parents. It will be studied in the years to come. Of comfort to the small circle of parents with young children around me is the following statement to the children: "When you grow up and have children, they will study the coronavirus in school. You will have personal stories to tell them."

Glossary

This glossary defines terms as used in the context of this book.

Adaptation: responsiveness to internal and external stresses and demands with the aim of personal wellbeing and optimal interpersonal outcomes

Attachment: the parent-child relationship bond that promotes the child's development and the parents' caretaking

Autobiographical narrative: life experiences organized into stories that include the personal meanings of lived events

Conflict: opposition within the mind between opposing wishes, values, impulses, and feelings

Consciousness: a mental state of awareness; the subjective experience of knowing

Continuity-of-self: a sense of self that is cohesive and constant throughout the past, present, and future, during fluctuating pleasurable and unpleasurable feelings, and varying external and internal changes

Denial: repudiation of an aspect of reality

Development: the process of physical and mental growth that includes the role of the environment; *see maturation*

Emotion regulation: the process of determining the expression of emotions, and the maintaining and returning to a state of equilibrium when intense feelings have been aroused that disrupt the equilibrium

Empathy: a process of feeling, imagining, thinking, or sensing the experience of another; central for all human relationships and vital for child development

Explicit memory: a memory that is organized into a narrative; *see implicit memory*

Good enough mother: a term coined by Donald Winnicott that refers to the mother providing sufficient amounts of gratification and frustration needed to promote healthy development

Historical truth: a reported occurrence that is verifiable; *see narrative truth*

Implicit memory: an emotion, bodily sensation, or interpersonal interaction that is connected to a past event and is re-experienced in the present; *see explicit memory*

Inner world: each person's subjective perceptions, thoughts, and feelings, including fantasies, wishes, and fears; the developing mental images of self, others, and self-with-other that preserve loving feelings and feelings of being loved when angry, frustrated, and disappointed

Insight: awareness of the underlying meaning of one's own behavior, thoughts, feelings, and memories, and those of others

Intergenerational trauma: the impact of events in one generation affecting subsequent generations

Inter-subjectivity: an interaction between two people where each is aware of the subjective experience of the other

Maturation: the unfolding of predetermined growth that lays the foundation for the emergence of more organized and complex physical and mental functions, and structures; *see development*

Mental representation: the ways in which the self, others, and self-with-other are symbolized in the mind

Narrative: a spoken account of a lived event that contains the personal meaning of the event including conscious and unconscious elements; recounted childhood memories are a narrative

Narrative truth: the personal meaning of a reported occurrence aiming toward internal conflict resolution and adaptation; *see historical truth*

Object permanence: the knowledge that things exist when they are not perceived

Psychoanalytic approach: exploration and interpretation of conscious and unconscious multiple meanings of behavior – actions, thoughts, feelings, wishes, memories, and fantasies

Rupture and repair: the universal fluctuation of loving and angry feelings in all parent-child relationships; term popularized by Ed Tronick; *see Suggested readings*

Self-reflection: contemplation of one's thoughts, feelings, and behavior from varying points of view

Sense of self: evolving thoughts and feelings about one's self that grow out of bodily, mental, and interpersonal experiences beginning in infancy

Shared memory narrative: parent-child co-created stories that help children to make sense of experience

Social referencing: babies' and toddlers' nonverbal signaling to their parents in order to get information to guide their responses when they are uncertain about the meaning of things, persons, situations, and inhibiting impulses, to share pleasures, and to support attachment

Trauma: the experience of being overwhelmed and unable to adapt

Treasured toy: described by Donald Winnicott as a transitional object; an object like a teddy bear or blanket to which a child creates a strong attachment, especially important during times of stress and separation from primary caretakers, and endows with emotion regulation capacities, that thereby promote the child's development of those needed mental capacities including emotion regulation, frustration tolerance, the ability to tolerate ambivalence, and the capacity to be alone

Unconscious: memories, thoughts, and feelings without awareness, which yet have influence

Unresolved trauma: ongoing feelings of anxiety, helplessness, and terror in response to past events

Suggested Readings

Anzieu-Premmereur, C. (2015). The Skin Ego: Dyadic Sensuality, Trauma in Infancy, and Adult Narcissistic Issues. *The Psychoanalytic Review*, 102(5), 659–682.

Beebe, B. (2014). *The Origins of Attachment: Infant Research and Adult Treatment*. London and New York: Routledge Press.

Beebe, B., Cohen, P., & Lachmann, F. (2016). *The Mother-Infant Interaction Picture Book*. New York: W.W. Norton & Company.

Beebe, B., Cohen, P., Sossin, M., & Markese, S. (Eds.) (2012). *Mothers, Infants and Young Children of September 11, 2001: A Primary Prevention Project*. London and New York: Routledge Press.

Coates, S. (2016). Can Babies Remember Trauma? Symbolic Forms of Representation in Traumatized Infants. *Journal of the American Psychoanalytic Association*, August 2016, 64, 751–776.

Fraiberg, S. (1959). *The Magic Years: Understanding and Handling the Problems of Early Childhood*. New York: Scribner.

Fraiberg, S. (1975). Ghosts in the Nursery: A Psychoanalytic Approach to the Problem of Impaired Infant-Mother Relationships. *Journal of the American Academy of Child Psychiatry*, 14, 387–421.

Fraiberg, S. (1980). *Clinical Studies in Infant Mental Health*. New York: Basic Books.

Gold, C. (2011). *Keeping Your Child in Mind*. Boston: Da Capo Lifelong Books.

Gold, C. (2016). *The Silenced Child*. Boston: Da Capo Lifelong Books.

Harris, A. (2015). *Ghosts in the Consulting Room*. London and New York: Routledge.

Lieberman, A. (2005). Angels in the Nursery. *Infant Mental Health Journal*, 26, 504–520.

Lieberman, A. (2017). *The Emotional Life of the Toddler*. New York: Simon and Schuster.

Lieberman, A. (2020). *Make Room for Baby*. New York and London: Guilford.

Miller, L., Kramer, R., Warner, V., Wickramaratne, P., & Weissman, M.M. (1997). The Intergenerational Transmission of Parental Bonding Among Women. *Journal of the American Academy of Child and Adolescent Psychiatry*, 36(8), 1134–1139.

Nachman, P. (1998). Maternal Identification: A Description of the Process in Real Time. *Journal of the American Psychoanalytic Association*, 46(1), 209–228.

Reiswig, R. (2011). Creating Space for Mourning a Lost Father and Husband After September 11: A Therapist's Reflections. *Journal of Infant, Child, and Adolescent Psychotherapy*, 10, 2–3, 238–241. DOI: 10.1080/15289168.2011.600128 [doi.org].

Scheftel, S. (2012). Why Aren't We Curious About Nannies? *The Psychoanalytic Study of the Child*, 66, 251–278.

Shapiro, T. (2011). Infant Psychiatry: Infants, Mothers and Dyads. *Journal of the American Academy of Child & Adolescent Psychiatry*, 50(3), 207–209.

Stern, D. (1996). *The Motherhood Constellation: A Unified View of Parent-Infant Psychotherapy*. New York: Basic Books.

Stern, D. (2000). *Interpersonal World of the Infant: A View from Psychoanalysis and Developmental Psychology*. New York: Basic Books.

Stern, D., & Brushweiler-Stern, N. (1998). *The Birth of a Mother: How the Motherhood Experience Changes You Forever*. New York: Basic Books.

Tronick, E., & Gold, C. (2020). *The Power of Discord*. New York: Little, Brown Spark.

Winnicott, D. (1953). Transitional Objects and Transitional Phenomena: A Study of the First Not-Me Possession. *International Journal of Psychoanalysis*, 34, 89–97.

Acknowledgments

For the past 20 years I had planned to write a book about my work: an everyday life *Ghosts in the Nursery*. I had almost given the idea up when I decided to write the book for my grandchildren. Watching my children be parents and the wonder of my grandchildren inspired me to write a memoire about my work. *Parenting and Childhood Memories* is an intergenerational story.

Family, close friends, and colleagues are essential for my work and for my wellbeing. I relied on them at every step to write this book. From vision to completion, I leaned on them heavily and am deeply grateful. Each one made a unique contribution. Children, teenagers, a composer, an artist, lawyers, pediatricians, social workers, psychologists, psychiatrists, and psychoanalysts: each provided a broadening perspective. *Parenting and Childhood Memories* would not have been possible without them.

I wish to thank **Kate Hawes**, **Hannah Wright** and the entire Routledge team for their collaboration, always supportive to publish the book I envisioned.

For over 20 years **Beatrice Beebe**, an esteemed infancy researcher and dear friend, urged me to write about my work. She helped me to highlight that useful insight is not only intellectual; it has a strong emotional component. After reading an early draft of my manuscript, she introduced me to Kate Hawes at Routledge, who submitted my manuscript for publication. **Susan Coates**, a close friend and expert on the intergenerational transmission of trauma, encouraged me from the beginning and added her scholarship and clinical experience to multiple drafts. **Aline Dasilva** supplied unending technical assistance, without which I was lost. In addition, her special talents with children lit up her editorial comments. **Suzanne Dikker**, a research psychologist, special friend, and young mother, provided thoughtful comments on an early manuscript draft that spanned literary grace, a grasp of psychological processes, and personal reflections that I relied on for support and to intensify my efforts. **Rick Finkelstein** provided an artist's eye. He enabled me to see more clearly the stories I was telling, and to describe the physical setting of each. **Claudia Gold**, a pediatrician on the faculty of the Boston Infant Mental Health Program and the author of *Keeping Your Child in Mind*, *The Silenced Child*, and *The Power of Discord*, provided me with her unwavering confidence to tell my story. While I surround myself with mental health professionals, **Toby Golick** and

Emily Jane Goodman, two close friends, brought their legal rigor to multiple drafts. **Edith Gould**'s years of friendship, psychoanalytic knowledge, and clinical wisdom helped me to deconstruct complex concepts and write them more clearly. **Beryl Kreisel** and I were best friends when our children were little. We know each other's ghosts and shared the magic of those early years of parenthood. I am deeply grateful for her comments. **Judith Levitan** is a dear friend and colleague. Her warm enthusiasm and support from dream to manuscript, combined with her clinical skill, honed manuscript drafts. **Steven Levitan** alerted me to the vivid memories adults have about their childhood treasured toys. **David Levine**'s literary acuity was valuable to organizing the raw material in early drafts. My esteemed colleague, my link to Selma Fraiberg, and new friend **Alicia Lieberman** challenged my ideas about ghosts in an intellectually rigorous and most generous way. Alicia's *Angels in the Nursery* and *The Emotional Life of the Toddler* are important classics that continue to influence my work. I am deeply admiring and grateful for her incisive comments and theoretical challenges, always with warm support. **Evelyn Lipper**, a developmental pediatrician, colleague, and friend, after hearing the letter to my grandchildren, suggested that I write a companion children's picture book. Her idea expanded and clarified my thinking. **Betsy Lynn**'s calm, reliable assistance, from beginning to end, kept manuscript details and drafts organized. When I hesitated, she always helped me to get on with it. **Alyson McCormick**, who has worked with me at the Center for over 20 years, helped to fill in gaps in order to create a richer and more accurate picture of my work. **Patricia Nachman**, whether in the middle of the night or at daybreak, first draft or twentieth, was always available to not only solve a writing problem, but to analyze it from every angle: developmental, theoretical, lexical, and semantic. **Wendy Olesker**'s careful read and thoughtful comments helped me to stay close to describing the complexity of my observations of what actually occurred and at the same time to convey the essence of what seemed to transpire – the magic of parent-child love. **Rita Reiswig**, co-director of the Anni Bergman Parent-Infant Program, a friend and colleague, greatly encouraged me by inviting me to present an excerpt from an early draft at their graduation. My sister, **Kathe Sackler**, and I share many childhood memories, but our ghosts are our own. We have learned about each other's ghosts, and when they emerge, we are respectful and supportive. Most memorable about her manuscript comments are those that demonstrated her appreciation of my description of being known and loved. **Susan Scheftel**, a close friend and colleague with a special talent for understanding the inner world of children, parents, writers, and readers, provided sensitive critiques of multiple drafts: always with support. **Theodore Shapiro**'s wealth of knowledge brought infant psychiatry to Weill Cornell. His enthusiastic endorsement of early drafts of *Parenting and Childhood Memories* convinced me, when uncertain, that I had stories to tell. **Lucy Simon**, a dear friend, composer, and lyricist, shared her magical musical thinking and helped me to find my voice. Early in my writing, **Meriamne Singer**, a psychiatrist, psychoanalyst, close friend, and colleague, helped me to keep in focus that both cherished and painful memories are essential for an organized, functioning inner world. Suzanne Singletary shared her art and architectural perspective helping me to sculpt my story. William Singletary, a most talented child psychiatrist and psychoanalyst who keeps magic and love central in his friendships and his work, inspired me. **Nadia Bruschweiler-Stern**, a pediatrician, child psychiatrist, co-author of *The Birth of a Mother,* and dear friend, generously shared her unique, attuned perspective on mothers and babies, and showered me with her personal love-magic. **Lissa Weinstein**, a writer and psychoanalyst, convinced me that I could write, and for long-enough moments, my self-consciousness vanished. **Myrna Weissman**'s support throughout this project was essential to me. In addition to her friendship, her extensive research, including the Intergenerational Study of Families, validates for me my anecdotal conclusions.

Ellie Becker, **Silvia Bonaventura**, **Laura Gonzales Conti**, **Eileen Jones**, **Colette Linnihan**, **Cleuzier Lopez**, **Maria Meigel**, **Gretchen Renner**, each contributed thoughtful comments that enriched the manuscript and my experience of writing it.

A special posthumous thank you to my friend and colleague **Daniel Stern** (1934–2012). He was the author of several books about child development and the early mother-child relationship, including *The Interpersonal World of the Infant*, *The Motherhood Constellation*, *Diary of a Baby*, *The First Relationship*, many scientific articles, and with his wife, Nadia Bruschweiler-Stern, *The Birth of a Mother.* In an unpublished 1992 pilot study, Dan and I applied his "breakfast interview" to mothers watching their toddlers play. We wanted to understand more about the architecture of ghosts popping into consciousness as mothers watch their toddlers. During a brief moment while observing their young children, we discovered that the mothers' childhood memories, both cherished and disturbing, were always triggered together.

After Dan's death in 2012, his widow, my close friend Nadia Bruschweiler-Stern, gave a small antique box to me that he had kept on his desk filled with pens, paper clips, and scraps of paper with brief notes. Now the box sits empty on my desk, but for me it holds the treasures of Dan's creative mind that are inspirational to me and contributed enormously to *Parenting and Childhood Memories*. In some ways, as for all adults, my childhood magical thinking continues.

In conclusion: special thanks to **Robert Michels**. After reading the first draft of *Parenting and Childhood Memories* he said, "You have a book."

With deepest gratitude I thank my children and grandchildren: **Jeff**, **Karen**, **Heather**, **Ben**, **Kaia**, **Isaac**, **Violet**, **Clio**, **and Evelyn**. They navigate my ghosts magnificently, surround me with joy, and fill me with contentment.

Index

Printed in Great Britain
by Amazon